EUROPEAN GLASS FURNISHINGS

FOR EASTERN PALACES

Jane Shadel Spillman

The Corning Museum of Glass, Corning, New York

TITLE PAGE

Design for chair, 1880s, from the Osler archives. Birmingham Museum and Art Gallery, Birmingham. The chair is similar to the one illustrated on the cover.

EDITOR
Richard W. Price

DESIGN AND TYPOGRAPHY
Jacolyn S. Saunders

PHOTOGRAPHIC SUPERVISOR
Nicholas L. Williams

PHOTOGRAPHIC ASSISTANT
Andrew M. Fortune

PROOFREADER
Joan M. Romano

REFERENCE LIBRARIAN
Gail P. Bardhan

RIGHTS AND REPRODUCTIONS
Jill Thomas-Clark

RESEARCHER
Mary B. Chervenak

Contents

Map of present-day India, showing cities
in which the palaces that house most of
the glass furniture discussed and illustrated in this book are located (red).
Other major cities are shown in yellow.

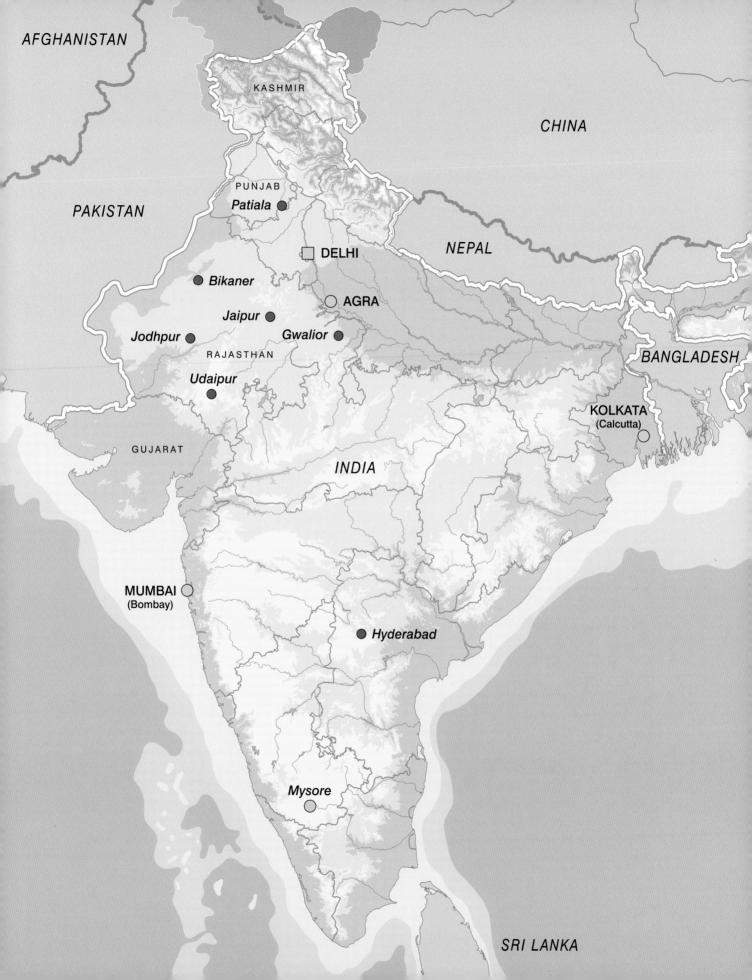

AFGHANISTAN

CHINA

PAKISTAN

KASHMIR

PUNJAB
Patiala

DELHI

NEPAL

Bikaner

AGRA

Jaipur

Gwalior

Jodhpur

RAJASTHAN

BANGLADESH

Udaipur

GUJARAT

INDIA

KOLKATA
(Calcutta)

MUMBAI
(Bombay)

Hyderabad

Mysore

SRI LANKA

Foreword

This book is an introduction to a remarkable episode in the history of glassmaking: the period in which rich and flamboyant rulers in the Indian subcontinent and the Middle East sought to possess large cut glass lighting devices and furniture, and European manufacturers encouraged and satisfied this desire. Although it had both precedents and sequels, the episode began in the 1840s, when a British manufacturer, F. & C. Osler of Birmingham, produced some of the first very large chandeliers and candelabra. The episode gathered momentum in the 1870s, when glass furniture began to receive increased attention, and it lasted until the 1920s.

Before the advent of strong and durable specialty glasses, most people thought of glass as an essentially fragile material. Even today, we tend to think of glass as an appropriate material for intricate lighting devices such as chandeliers with multitudes of prisms, but the notion of usable glass furniture before the introduction of high-tech glasses strikes us as almost paradoxical. The episode described here began with delicate chandeliers, proceeded with the production of ever larger lighting devices and fountains, and ended with the application of the techniques of making large lighting devices to the manufacture of sturdy, richly cut furniture.

Since at least Roman times, glass has occasionally been used for furniture and architectural ornament. A large cameo glass fragment in The Metropolitan Museum of Art, New York, is believed to be part of a first-century C.E. tabletop. Louis XIV of France (r. 1643–1715) owned a table with an elaborate mosaic glass top and glass-covered legs, and Catherine the Great of Russia ordered glass fixtures and glass-topped tables for her palace at Tsarskoye Selo in 1780–1783.

Catherine's taste for glass furniture set a style at the Russian court, and in the early 19th century, the Imperial Glassworks in St. Petersburg manufactured numerous glass lamps and candelabra, as well as glass and gilt-bronze furniture, for the palaces of the czars. Some of these objects contained very large glass elements. The

Imperial Glassworks even made a glass bed with elaborate fixtures (including fountains) that Czar Alexander I presented to Shah Fath Ali of Persia in 1824.

At about the same time, French glassmakers began to produce large fixtures and furniture. By 1814, Philippe-Auguste Charpentier, a Parisian glass seller and engraver, had named his gallery L'Escalier de Cristal (The Glass Staircase) and installed a signature glass staircase at the entrance. Five years later, a group of glass candelabra, tables, and other furniture won a gold medal at the Fifth French Industrial Exhibition and was snapped up by an international clientele that included Russian and Spanish royalty and the Persian ambassador.

F. & C. Osler was probably the first European glass manufacturer to recognize the huge potential of the Eastern market for spectacular glass objects. In 1840, Osler began to display chandeliers in a store in Calcutta, India; in 1843, the firm established its own sales representative there; and shortly afterward, it opened its own Calcutta showroom—all before opening a shop in London. Four years later, Osler received a commission from Ibrahim Pasha, the heir to the Ottoman throne, to supply a pair of cut glass candelabra, 17 feet tall, for the tomb of Muhammad at Medina.

The dramatic increase in the scale and scope of cut glass in the first half of the 19th century was demonstrated conclusively at the Great Exhibition of the Works of Industry of All Nations, held in London in 1851. The exhibition was housed in a gigantic greenhouse, the Crystal Palace, and it contained monumental examples of cut glass. Osler displayed a working glass fountain 27 feet high that was regarded as "perhaps the most striking object in the Exhibition."[1] The company also showed a pair of candelabra, eight feet high, that had been purchased by Prince Albert for Queen Victoria in 1848. In the same exhibition, the London firm of Apsley Pellatt and Company displayed a large, multicolored chandelier with decoration based on architectural ornament in the medieval Alhambra palace in Spain, the source of much of the "Moorish" decoration favored in Europe in the mid- and later 19th century.

The Great Exhibition and subsequent world's fairs, such as the London exhibition of 1862 and the Paris expositions of 1855, 1867, and 1878, were showcases for other manufacturers of large-scale cut glass objects. These manufacturers included Jonas Defries & Sons, W. P. and G. Phillips, and Lloyd and Summerfield in England, and the Compagnie des Verreries et Cristalleries de Baccarat and the Cristallerie de Pantin in France.

During the second and third quarters of the 19th century, a variety of factors facilitated European trade with the East. The British and Ottoman governments signed a trade agreement in 1838, Britain and France entered into an alliance with Turkey in the Crimean War in 1856, India came under direct British rule in 1859, and the opening of the Suez Canal in 1869 greatly shortened maritime journeys between Europe and much of Asia.

These political and economic developments, combined with the excitement generated by the world's fairs, provided European manufacturers with new opportunities to market large cut glass objects overseas. When the Ottoman sultan Abdülmecid I constructed his Dolmabahçe Palace in Istanbul in 1853–1856, he employed a prominent French architect (Charles Séchan, who also designed the Paris Opera House) and commissioned sets of prismatic mirrors, each of which was 15 feet high and contained 1,000 prisms, from Defries & Sons. The palace also featured a staircase with glass banisters, together with cut glass chandeliers, candelabra, and fireplaces.

Meanwhile, the Turkish viceroy in Egypt ordered chandeliers and candelabra from Baccarat, and Shah Nāṣer od-Dīn of Persia also awarded Baccarat a large contract for lighting devices in 1873.

While chandeliers and candelabra formed spectacular displays at the Great Exhibition and all subsequent 19th-century world's fairs, little cut glass furniture was in evidence before the Paris exposition of 1878. However, at the London exhibition of 1862, Lloyd and Summerfield displayed "glass . . . legs for pianofortes, tables, &c, for use in hot climates, where wood is liable to the ravages of the white ant."[2] This was an unexpected insight into the practical value of glass furniture in tropical and subtropical regions.

At the 1878 exposition, Osler, Baccarat, and Pantin all exhibited glass furniture. Writing of one display, a critic observed: "There is a splendid crystal chair of state and footstool. The framework is of cut glass, arranged in skilfully devised patterns, glittering like a mass of gems, which will attract the notice of many of the Eastern potentates who visit the Exhibition."[3]

Prophetic words! The almost instant success of furniture production by Osler, Baccarat, and other glassmakers is illustrated by orders from three Indian rulers. When Jayaji Rao Scindia built the Jai Vilas Palace at Gwalior shortly before the visit of the Prince of Wales in 1875–1876, he ordered two of the largest chandeliers ever constructed by Osler (each was 40 feet tall), but no furniture. On the other hand, when the maharana Sajjan Singh and his successor, Fateh Singh, commissioned Osler to supply the City Palace at Udaipur, beginning in 1878, they ordered tables, chairs, settees, a bed, and numerous other glass objects—the largest collection of glass furniture in the world. And in 1894, the nizam of Hyderabad ordered a large set of cut glass furniture from a company in Kamenický Šenov, Bohemia: Elias Palme. Although Palme had no experience in the making of glass furniture, he accepted the challenge. After successfully producing a table and a chair, he signed a huge contract to supply all manner of items, from tables and double beds to fountains and swings, but not a single chandelier.

This book, therefore, tells the story of how the European taste for cut glass chandeliers and candelabra took hold in India and the Middle East, and led in the late 1870s to the development of a novel range of cut glass furniture made by European companies almost exclusively for Eastern customers.

David Whitehouse
Executive Director
The Corning Museum of Glass

Glass Furniture in the 19th Century

TODAY, IT IS NOT at all unusual to find glass tables and cabinets, as well as large glass lighting devices. But in the second half of the 19th century, when glass was first used in furniture on a commercial basis, it would have been truly remarkable to see such objects. The development of glass furniture was dependent, first of all, upon advances in glassmaking technology. During the 19th century, glassmakers learned how to blow or cast relatively large pieces and anneal them so that they would be strong enough to withstand the pressure of cutting tools. This enabled them to manufacture ornately decorated supports for massive candelabra and large, thick slabs of glass that could be used as tabletops. Some such pieces were used in glass fountains and furniture.

Even before that time, however, individual pieces of furniture had been decorated with glass tops or glass inlays, but these were never in standard production. Instead, they were usually one-of-a-kind pieces made for royalty or for the very wealthy, and they were often created in state-operated glasshouses. Wooden objects lavishly decorated with glass are known from the late 17th century, when Louis XIV owned a table with a mosaic glass top and glass legs, probably made in Italy (Fig. 1-1). Lady Mary Wortley Montagu (1689–1762), the indefatigable English traveler, described a set of glass-decorated furniture that she saw for sale in Venice in 1756. She noted, "It is impossible to imagine their beauty; they deserve being placed in a prince's dressing-room, or grand cabinet. . . ."[1] Catherine II of Russia had glass walls, doors, arches, columns, and pilasters designed by Charles Cameron for three private rooms in the Grand Palace at Tsarskoye Selo in 1780–

Figure 1-2

1783 (Fig. 1-2). There were also tables decorated with blue and opaline glass, several with *églomisé*[2] tops (Fig. 1-3). A few of these are still in Catherine's palace, although the opaline glass architectural features were destroyed during World War II and can be seen only in paintings of the period.[3]

The production of glass furniture in Russia began in the early 19th century, when the Imperial Glassworks fashioned pieces for the imperial family. Two surviving examples are a pair of tables that have tops consisting of a single octagonal slab of blue glass, a center section of blown amber glass with swirling cut channels, and a cast square base of amber glass so thick that it appears to be black. Gilded bronze was used to hold the sides of the tabletop together and to fasten the central support to the top and bottom, but the tables are essentially made of glass. They were designed in 1808 by Thomas-Jean de Thomon (1754–1813), a French architect who was also the chief designer at the Imperial factory. One of these tables, with its original washbasin and pitcher of blue and colorless cut glass, is still in the Pavlovsk Palace outside St. Petersburg. It is thought to have been made for Czar Alexander I to present to his mother, the widow of Paul I. The other is in the collection of The Corning Museum of Glass (Fig. 1-4). It, too, may have been a gift from Alexander to his mother, or he may have given it to his sister. In the late 19th century, this table was probably taken by the empress Maria Fyodorovna (1847–1928), the widow of Alex-

Figure 1-3

Mahogany writing table with top and side panels made of painted and gilded glass; gilded bronze mounts. Attributed to Heinrich Gambs and Jonathan Ott, St. Petersburg, Russia, about 1795. Hillwood Museum & Gardens, Washington, D.C. (32.31).

FIGURE 1-4

Glass table with gilded bronze mounts. Designed by Thomas-Jean de Thomon in 1808 and made at the Imperial Glassworks, St. Petersburg, Russia. H. 79 cm. The Corning Museum of Glass, Corning, New York (74.3.129), purchased with funds from the Museum Endowment Fund.

ander III, to Denmark (she was originally Princess Dagmar of Denmark). It was used in the palace at Hvidore Castle, where the Russian imperial family stayed during their visits to that country. Eventually, it was placed on the antiques market.

The Imperial Glassworks also provided a number of large standing vases and lamps for the royal palaces. Many of these objects combined colored and colorless cut glass, often with ormolu (gilded metal) handles and pedestals. Several candelabra with pillars of blue glass made by the Potemkin glasshouse can still be found in the former royal palaces. The Imperial factory produced very large vases supported on tripod bases, as well as massive ruby or colorless vases with ormolu handles (Fig. 1-5). Although Russian decorative arts were often influenced by French designs, nothing like any of these pieces was being made elsewhere in Europe at that time.

An even more remarkable piece of Russian furniture was the glass bed made for the shah of Persia in 1824. Five years earlier, Czar Alexander I had sent the shah a crystal (colorless lead glass) basin as a diplomatic gift. The shah was so pleased that he requested a glass bed to go with the basin, and the czar consented to order this at a cost of about 50,000 rubles. The bed was designed by Ivan Alexeyevich Ivanov (1779–1848), chief designer at the Imperial Glassworks, where it was made. The original sketch of the bed survives, along with a description by Lieutenant Noskov, the Russian official who transported the object to Tehran and installed it for the shah in

1826–1827.[4] It consisted of an iron frame plated with silver and brass and then covered with cut crystal. There were crystal columns at the corners and a crystal headboard that rested on a platform of turquoise glass. Seven crystal vases surrounding the bed were actually fountains. As far as we know, this was the first piece of European glass furniture made for an Eastern monarch. Although glass originated in the Middle East, very little of it was being made there in the 19th century.

At about the same time, the French were creating cut glass furniture that was even more elaborate than the objects made in Russia, although their glass was entirely colorless. The restoration of the monarchy and the accession of Louis XVIII in 1814 popularized luxury wares and resulted in an increase in both the quantity and the quality of French-produced glass items. The furniture and accessories of this period (1814–1848) were often influenced by classical designs. They include porcelain vases from the Sèvres factory, sphinx-like figures that were used as supports in both porcelain and furniture, and classically styled profiles as decorative motifs. Gothic motifs were also popular.[5]

On April 22, 1813, the glass engraver Philippe-Auguste Charpentier (1781–1815) applied to the Consulting Committee for Arts and Manufactures for a *brevet d'invention* (letters patent) permitting him to employ glass in the manufacture of furniture. The committee replied that this process could not be protected by a patent, and there is no record that such a grant was issued.[6] At that time, Charpentier was the proprietor of a business in the Palais-Royal that would be named L'Escalier de Cristal (The Glass Staircase) by 1814. Some pieces of finely engraved glass have been attributed to this shop, which probably employed several engravers.[7] It had a much-admired glass staircase at its entrance that was probably the first of its kind.[8] Despite the lack of a patent, Charpentier must have persisted in seeking to make glass furniture. A letter from his sister, Marie-Jeanne-Rosalie Désarnoud-Charpentier, who managed L'Escalier de Cristal, to the royal household reports that "dans ce moment je termine un nouveau meuble tout en cristal" (at this moment, I am finishing a new piece of furniture that is all glass).[9] Her shop later produced a cut glass dressing table and matching armchair for the Fifth French Industrial Exhibition, which was held at the Louvre in 1819. The glass parts for this display were supplied by Aimé-Gabriel d'Artigues (1778–1848). He was the manager of the Compagnie des Verreries et Cristalleries de Baccarat in France (a position that he had assumed in 1816) as well as a glasshouse in Vonêche, Belgium. Although it is impossible to know which of his two factories produced the glass, Baccarat seems more likely because D'Artigues was unable to import his glass from Vonêche after February 1818.

In any event, Mme Désarnoud-Charpentier and L'Escalier de Cristal won a gold medal and considerable acclaim for this exhibit, which consisted of six pieces. The catalog describes them as "meubles de cristal, savoir: 1. Une toilette de cristal décorée de bronzes dorés et des meubles qui en dépendent; 2. Une cheminée décorée de bronzes dorés et cristaux; 3. Deux grands candelabres de cristal et bronzes dorés; 4. Deux tables ornés de bronzes et cristal; 5. Une grande pendule et plusieurs grands vases ornés de cristal et bronze; et 6. plus, toutes les pièces qui garnissent ordinairement ces divers meubles" (glass furniture, including 1. a dressing table decorated with

FIGURE 1-5

Vase of ruby glass, blown, overlaid, cut, polished; gilded bronze mounts. Russia, St. Petersburg, Imperial Glassworks, about 1829, possibly made for the First Industrial Exposition of that year. H. 56 cm. The Corning Museum of Glass, Corning, New York (96.3.22).

Meubles et Ornemens en Cristal.

gilt bronze and the furniture that belongs with it; 2. a mantelpiece decorated with bronze and glass; 3. two large candelabra of glass with bronze decoration; 4. two tables decorated with bronze and crystal; 5. a great clock and several large vases decorated with glass and bronze; and 6. all the pieces that are necessary to decorate these pieces of furniture).[10] Accounts of the exhibition also mention that her customers included the Persian ambassador, the royal families of Russia and Spain, and "la Reine d'Etrurie,"[11] who was probably María-Luisa, daughter of Charles IV of Spain. She was the former queen of Etruria, and she was known as the duchess of Lucca in 1815.[12] Another document characterizes the display as "toutes les garnitures, resplendissent de l'éclat du diamant" (all the fittings shine with the brilliance of a diamond).[13]

From these accounts, it is not clear who purchased the dressing table. Marie-Caroline, the duchess of Berry and a daughter of the king, bought a table, chair, and tea table soon thereafter. These objects remained in the collection at her château in Rosny until it was sold in 1836.[14] However, María Luisa Teresa of Parma, wife of Charles IV, is recorded as purchasing a *toilette en crystal* (glass dressing table) for 16,000 francs at the exhibition, so we cannot be sure which of these two royal ladies acquired the dressing table. The design for the table (Fig. 1-6a) was published by Julia Fontanelle in 1829,[15] and an example (Fig. 1-6b) matching the design that surfaced in a private collection in 1947 is now in the Louvre.

FIGURE 1-6A

Design for dressing table. From *Nouveau manuel complet du verrier....*, published by Julia Fontanelle in Paris, 1829, pl. 3. Juliette K. and Leonard S. Rakow Research Library of The Corning Museum of Glass, Corning, New York.

FIGURE 1-6B

Dressing table and chair. Made at L'Escalier de Cristal, Paris, 1819. H. (table) 169 cm. Musée du Louvre, Paris (OA11229; OA11230).

FIGURE 1-7

Dressing table. Made at
L'Escalier de Cristal, Paris,
1819–1830. H. 118.1 cm. Newport Restoration Foundation,
Newport, Rhode Island
(1999.508).

FIGURE 1-8

Table with three-part cut
glass base. Probably made at
L'Escalier de Cristal, Paris,
1819–1830. H. 83.8 cm. Aveline, Paris.

Like the Russian pieces, the French table and chair are supported on glass parts, although they also have metal fittings that connect the glass. The dressing table in the Louvre has an *églomisé* top, as well as cut glass supports for the mirror that also hold three candles each. Gilded bronze figures of Flora, the Roman goddess of flowers, and Zephyrus, the personification of the west wind, are merely decorative, not structural. The cut glass supports for the back of the chair are in the form of dolphins, and they match the table legs. The chair also has two cut glass legs and a massive square cut glass base. The designer of this tour de force is thought to have been Nicolas Henri Jacob (1782–1871), a student of the painter Jacques Louis David (1748–1825). A very similar table (Fig. 1-7), undoubtedly also from L'Escalier de Cristal and of the same date, has an oval mirror and candle holders (they were electrified in the 1950s) supported by bronze cupids, a rectangular glass top, four straight legs of cut glass, and diagonal glass supports that are like the vertical supports on the other table. Both tables have a flat center drawer. The latter example was in the United States for most of the 20th century. It was in the collection of the late Doris Duke in Newport, Rhode Island, who had acquired it in 1959 from the estate of Thelma Chrysler Foy. This table carries an attribution maintaining that it came from Malmaison, the home of Empress Joséphine. However, because the empress died in 1814, it cannot have belonged to her. It seems likely that the table matching Fontanelle's drawing was purchased by the queen of Spain and the other belonged to the duchess of Berry, but it is impossible to be more specific.

Five smaller tables with cut glass supports and a cut glass base or top are also known. Three are in the Spanish royal collection in Madrid,[16] while the fourth is in a collection in Paris (Fig. 1-8). Another was sold at Sotheby's New York gallery in 1982.[17] All are slightly different in design. L'Escalier de Cristal probably made these tables to order for special customers, and one or more of them may be the smaller tables that were mentioned as no. 4 in the account of the 1819 French exhibition quoted above. At the same fair, a pair of candelabra nearly 10 feet tall also won a prize. These signed objects, each of which featured a marble base, a bronze and cut glass standard, and six glass arms, were made at the factory of Chagot Frères at Mont Cenis.[18] The cutting is very similar to that on the furniture from L'Escalier de Cristal, and had these pieces not been signed by another manufacturer, they could well have been attributed to that shop. Although some other French firms may have been making large lighting devices at that time, it is unlikely that any of them were producing furniture. Therefore, if more glass furniture

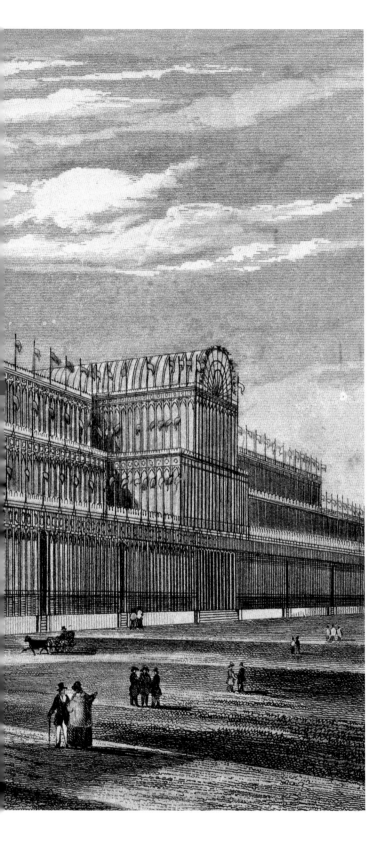

FIGURE 1-9

Watercolor design for the Crystal Palace, London. Joseph Paxton, 1850. Juliette K. and Leonard S. Rakow Research Library of The Corning Museum of Glass, Corning, New York.

of this type is discovered, it can be attributed to L'Escalier de Cristal.

All of these objects were originally designed to be shown at industrial expositions, which became increasingly important as showcases for manufactured goods in Europe. They provided a forum in which companies from various nations could display the best of their wares. The more elaborate displays drew considerable attention from visitors and critics alike. It was here that many potential customers got their first glimpse of glass furniture.

In 1851, the scale of these exhibitions changed from regional to global. The Great Exhibition of the Works of Industry of All Nations was the first of more than a dozen world's fairs that were held in various countries during the second half of the 19th century. The Great Exhibition was opened by Queen Victoria in Hyde Park, London, on May 1. Gaily costumed representatives of foreign nations and British possessions attended the opening ceremony and praised the displays. The number and size of the exhibits—and the remarkable Crystal Palace, the glass structure that housed them all (Fig. 1-9)—were staggering in their effect. The British press was ecstatic, and visitors flocked to see the magnificent building and its contents. The Crystal Palace made architectural and engineering history. It was designed by Joseph Paxton, estate manager and one-time gardener to the duke of Devonshire. Paxton had designed greenhouses, but no glass structure on the scale of this one had previously been envisioned, much less erected. The building was nicknamed the "Crystal Palace" by *Punch* magazine, and to everyone's astonishment, it was completed in just 17 weeks.

The principal exhibitors of glass lighting devices and furniture at the 19th-century world's fairs were F. & C. Osler of Birmingham (England), Jonas Defries & Sons of London, and the Baccarat firm of France. Their displays are discussed in chapters 3, 4, and 6 respectively. The excitement generated by these display pieces prompted other companies to create such works. For example, the 1851 exhibition included a "large chandelier of white[,] ruby and blue glass, in the style of [the] Alhambra," which was shown by Apsley Pellatt and Company.[19] The Alhambra is a Moorish palace in Spain. Originally built in the 11th century just outside Granada by the Muslim conquerors of southern Spain, it was enlarged and decorated in the 13th and 14th centuries. Its tiles and other decoration are very elaborate and colorful. The English architect Owen Jones (1809–1874), who had a profound influence on British design in the mid-19th century, published a book about the Alhambra in 1842, and it was illustrated with his own drawings. Although the book was not particularly popular at that time, it did succeed in drawing the attention of the British art world to the building. Eventually, the Alhambra became a symbol of the mysterious Middle East to the British and American public, and colorful glass was often described as being in the style of the Alhambra.

Pellatt's chandelier was designed to capture some of the splendor of the Alhambra itself. This was the only colored piece in the firm's display, which included several chandeliers. Unfortunately, it was not illustrated in the exhibition catalog. Colored chandeliers were not fashionable, and none of the reporters commented on this piece, which was clearly ahead of its time. At the next London world's fair, held in 1862, one critic commented, "We are glad to observe that this and other firms do not perpetuate the error observable in the glass exhibition of 1851, of making chandeliers of coloured glass; for nothing can surpass the iridescent lustre of pure colourless flint glass."[20]

The 1862 exhibition featured a glass table made by the London glass decorating company of W. P. and G. Phillips (Fig. 1-10). Its decoration was blown rather than cut, and its center pillar and three feet were curving and fluid. This was characteristic of the new and popular Anglo-Venetian style. The glass blanks for this table had been made by Thomas Webb & Sons of Stourbridge. The table, which was 26 inches high, was made in four pieces, and it had no metal parts. It attracted much favorable attention from the critics, and it was illustrated in J. B. Waring's three-volume report on the exposition. This was the first piece of glass furniture made by a British firm. It does not seem to have inspired any copies, however, and it would be nearly 20 years before more glass furniture was made either in France or in England.

Another exhibitor at the 1862 world's fair was the London firm of Lloyd and Summerfield, which displayed "glass bars for windows, aquariums, . . . legs for pianofortes, tables, &c, for use in hot climates, where wood is liable to the ravages of the white ant."[21] Unfortunately, no picture or further description of these table legs has been found.

Large lighting devices were exhibited at the 1855 and 1867 Expositions Universelles in Paris, but there was nothing groundbreaking except for Baccarat's immense glass fountain in 1867. However, the next exposition held in Paris, in 1878, featured the largest glass objects ever displayed at a world's fair. The most impressive of these pieces was a 16-foot-high temple made by Baccarat (this is discussed in chapter 6). A rival French firm, the Cristallerie de Pantin, presented, in addition to its cut and engraved tableware, an item described in the jury reports as a "guéridon formé de trois parties de grande dimension, sans aucun ajustage en metal" (small glass table made in three parts, without any metal supports).[22] In 1880, Pantin gave this table to the Conservatoire des Arts et Métiers, where it was broken in 1900. Unfortunately, no illustration of the piece survives. Osler also showed glass furniture at the 1878 fair, including a cabinet (see page 70) and a chair.

The Paris expositions of 1889 and 1900 included extensive glass exhibits by companies from around the world, but they did not rival the displays of 1878 in size or in their ability to impress visitors. Having demonstrated the type of cut glass furniture they could produce, Baccarat and Osler concentrated on selling it rather than producing it for exhibitions.

FIGURE 1-10

Glass table in a print, "Engraved and Coloured Glass by Messrs. W. P. & G. Phillips, London." From *Masterpieces of Industrial Art & Sculpture at the International Exhibition, 1862* [chapter 3, note 8], pl. 68. Juliette K. and Leonard S. Rakow Research Library of The Corning Museum of Glass, Corning, New York.

The Eastern Connection

IN THE 19TH CENTURY, at the very time when glassmakers were improving their skill in fashioning and annealing the large pieces that would be needed to create furniture, the number of contacts between Europe and countries to the east was increasing, and both England and France were expanding their empires to the east. Many European manufacturers were seeking world markets, and many Asian countries were eager for Western goods. In the latter half of the century, several glass companies began to make large, colored objects—including chandeliers, candelabra, fountains, and furniture—that were specifically designed for the very wealthy rulers of the Near East and India.

Sultans Mahmud II (r. 1808–1839) and his son Abdülmecid I (r. 1839–1861) wanted to open the shrinking Ottoman Empire to European trade. A trade agreement was signed by the Ottoman and British governments in 1838, and shortly after his accession to the throne, Abdülmecid promulgated a reformed dress code that banned the turban in favor of the more modern fez. In 1839, he instituted the Tanzimat reforms, which modernized schools and the Turkish infrastructure, and during his reign he built roads and railroads to make the country more accessible. In 1856, Turkey was allied with England and France against Russia during the Crimean War. Abdülmecid's brother and successor, Abdülaziz (r. 1861–1876), visited Europe as the first Ottoman sultan to leave Turkey on a peaceful mission. In 1867, at the invitation of Napoleon III, he traveled to Paris to visit the world's fair, and then he went to London, where he was received by Queen Victoria.

In embracing modernity and Western ideas, Abdülmecid decided to move from the Topkapi Palace in Istanbul to a new palace constructed in a Western architectural style. This was Istanbul's Dolmabahçe Palace (Figs. 2-1 and 2-2), which was built between 1853 and 1856. Its Turkish features, such as its dome, are combined with a wide range of European motifs, including triangular pediments. The decoration was designed by Charles Séchan (1803–1874), the Frenchman who created the new Paris Opera House. The palace also contained a considerable number of large lighting fixtures and other glass objects. Among them was a fantastic set of eight mirrors produced by the London firm of Jonas Defries & Sons (Fig. 2-3).

The best description of these mirrors, which are still housed in the palace, comes from a publication of the 1862 world's fair in London, where Defries exhibited one of them. It noted that "the greatest curiosity" in this firm's display

THE SULTAN'S DINING SALOON AT THE PALACE OF DOLMA-BAGTCHE.

FIGURE 2-1

View of the Dolmabahçe Palace, Istanbul, built in Western style, 1853–1856.

FIGURE 2-2

Print showing the sultan's dining room in the Dolmabahçe Palace. From *The Illustrated News of the World*, January 28, 1860, p. 60. Juliette K. and Leonard S. Rakow Research Library of The Corning Museum of Glass, Corning, New York.

FIGURE 2-3

Prismatic mirror, one of eight in the Dolmabahçe Palace. Made by Jonas Defries & Sons, London, about 1856–1862.

is the Prismatic Mirror, one of eight designed and manufactured for the Sultan of Turkey, to adorn two of the principal saloons of the Imperial Palace on the Bosphorus. The apartments in question are called the Saloon Mehben and the Saloon Zwhlbech, the walls of which, on the side overlooking the Bosphorus, are of circular form. Both are furnished in the European style, with stoves and lofty mantelpieces; but a great difficulty arose in fitting the curved space over the fire-place with mirrors, as it was impossible to make mirrors of such a form and of the immense size required. To overcome this difficulty, which for a time was considered almost insurmountable, Messrs. Defries and Sons designed the prismatic mirrors. . . . Each of the Sultan's saloons is to be decorated with four of these mirrors, fifteen feet high by eight broad, and containing 1,000 prisms. All the prisms join each other at the sides, so as to form almost one piece, and at the ends are dovetailed together, and held into the frame by a system of copper rods, which fit into grooves cast in the glass. By this means the mirror is made concave, to suit the form of the wall. The weight of pure crystal glass in each mirror is one ton, and the weight of the metal back is one ton more. They will[,] of course, be dispatched to the Bosphorus in pieces, and on arrival at their destination the backs of the prisms will be silvered, and all put together—each mirror in a gilt Turkish frame of great breadth and richness. To show the effect, one has been silvered and put together at Messrs. Defries' warehouse; and the play of colour and brilliancy of light reflected upon the whole mass of prisms is something inconceivably beautiful. In the palace, the mirrors will be placed opposite each other, with a hundred-branched light before each. . . . The whole design, arrangement, and manufacture of the mirrors reflect the very highest credit upon the enterprise and skill of Messrs. Defries; and from the interest which has been evinced in them since their exhibition, there seems little doubt that, in spite of their great cost, they will soon become fashionable enrichments in the palaces of the wealthy.[1]

Another publication, however, described this same mirror as "singularly ugly and of equally bad taste."[2] Good taste was considered to be one of the most important criteria for judging "art manufactures," which modern critics call the decorative arts.

Defries registered the design for the prismatic mirror on May 14, 1857, and it was probably supplied to the palace that year. Thus it was not new when Defries displayed it at the 1862 fair. However, because it afforded a unique solution to the problem presented by the design of the space in which it was to be located, the company was justifiably proud of it.

Another remarkable design from the Dolmabahçe Palace is a staircase with glass banisters (Fig. 2-4a, b) that must have been installed during its construction. The design for this staircase (Fig. 2-4c, d) was registered by the London chandelier makers Hancock, Rixon and Dunt on March 12, 1852. There are two slightly different versions of the staircase in the records of The National Archives U.K., but both of them

FIGURE 2-4A

Staircase with glass banisters at the Dolmabahçe Palace. Made by Hancock, Rixon and Dunt, London, 1853–1856.

European Glass Furnishings for Eastern Palaces

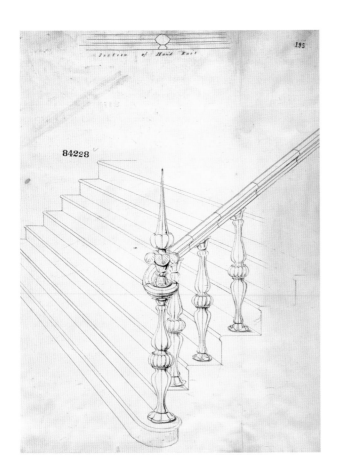

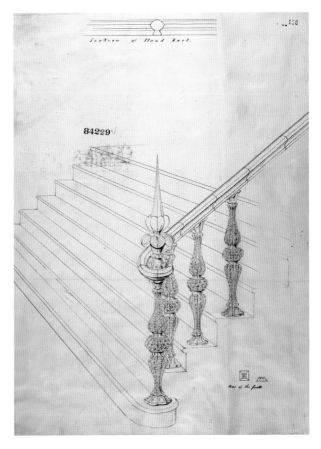

Figure 2-4b

Detail of glass banisters shown in Figure 2-4a.

Figure 2-4c

Design for glass banisters like those at Dolmabahçe Palace. Registered by Hancock, Rixon and Dunt, March 12, 1852. The National Archives U.K. (tna(pro) bt43/60 84228).

Figure 2-4d

Design for glass banisters like those at Dolmabahçe Palace. Registered by Hancock, Rixon and Dunt, March 12, 1852. The National Archives U.K. (tna(pro) bt43/60 84229).

were registered on the same day. According to one modern historian, "The manufacture of a baluster of this kind, which entailed joining together a number of quite separately produced individual pieces, was a matter of no great difficulty, but its importance lay in the choice and simple but effective realisation of a design that would introduce something utterly new to the architectural setting."[3]

The palace's 285 rooms were illuminated by 82 chandeliers (52 of them were made of glass) and nearly 400 candelabra, including 60 glass examples. Although the palace was not yet under construction in 1851, some of the glass is supposed to have been purchased at London's Great Exhibition, the first world's fair, which was held that year. Turkey had sent displays to this fair, so it would have been surprising if Turkish officials had not brought back furnishings from London. Indeed, the influence of the exposition can be seen in the fact that there was a glass fountain in the palace similar to the one that had been shown at the Crystal Palace, although it was smaller (Fig. 2-5). At most of the subsequent world's fairs, Turkey presented displays of traditional crafts and its developing technology.

Hancock, Rixon and Dunt also supplied the palace with a mammoth chandelier containing 644 lights, which hangs in the throne room. It is signed by the firm and dated "June 1853" on the metalwork. This chandelier weighs four and a half tons, and the design for this object, or a very similar one, was registered on October 21, 1851

FIGURE 2-5

Conservatory with glass
fountain at the Dolmabahçe
Palace. Probably made by F.
& C. Osler, Birmingham,
England, 1860s or 1870s. The
lighting devices are probably
also from Osler, but the small
glass stand at the far right
was made by the Compagnie
des Verreries et Cristalleries
de Baccarat, probably in the
1880s.

Figure 2-6

Design for a chandelier. Registered by Hancock, Rixon and Dunt, October 21, 1851. The National Archives U.K. (TNA(PRO) BT43/60 81056).

Figure 2-7

Design for a glass fireplace. Registered by Hancock, Rixon and Dunt, March 3, 1852. The National Archives U.K. (TNA(PRO) BT43/60 84128).

Figure 2-8

Design for a glass fireplace. Registered by Hancock, Rixon and Dunt, March 3, 1852. The National Archives U.K. (TNA(PRO) BT43/60 84129).

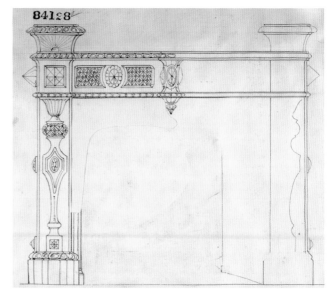

FIGURE 2-9A

Glass fireplace in the Dolmabahçe Palace. Probably
made by Hancock, Rixon
and Dunt, 1853.

FIGURE 2-9B

Detail of fireplace.

(Fig. 2-6). According to palace records, this was a gift to the sultan from Queen Victoria. The firm also registered two designs for glass fireplaces (Figs. 2-7 and 2-8) on March 3, 1852, just a few days before the banisters were registered. These are thought to have been made for the palace. There are four glass fireplaces in the corners of the entrance hall, four more in a reception room, and two made of red glass in the small audience chamber (Fig. 2-9a, b). Although the fireplaces in the palace are not a perfect match for the registered designs, many elements are similar, and it therefore seems probable that Hancock, Rixon and Dunt created the fireplaces (Fig. 2-9c–f).

More than 100 large glass lighting pieces are housed in the Dolmabahçe Palace. At least two of them are Venetian, and others are clearly French. However, ruby-cased chandeliers that were probably made by the English firm of F. & C. Osler are

Figure 2-9c

Detail of fireplace.

Figure 2-9d

Glass fireplace in the Dolmabahçe Palace. Probably made by Hancock, Rixon and Dunt, 1853.

FIGURE 2-9F

Detail of fireplace.

FIGURE 2-9E

Glass fireplace in the Dolmabahçe Palace. Probably made by Hancock, Rixon and Dunt, 1853.

found in the Halife Staircase, the Blue Salon, and the dowager sultana's reception room, and there are several Osler candelabra in the palace. The Beylerbeyi Palace in Istanbul also has Osler lighting, including a large green-cased chandelier and a candelabrum.

Finally, the Dolmabahçe Palace has a glass piano made by Gaveau of Paris about 1900. The piano was encased in glass for no conceivable functional reason, but probably just to inspire amazement. Today, it is displayed with a glass chair that was made in the 1890s by the Bohemian firm of Elias Palme (see page 133). Although these two objects were produced in different countries, they were probably purchased at the same time.

Most of the furniture for the Dolmabahçe Palace was ordered during and shortly after its construction, although new pieces were periodically added later in the 19th century. Istanbul's Beylerbeyi and Çirağan Palaces were built shortly after the Dolmabahçe Palace, and they evince a similar Western influence and use of glass.[4] All of these palaces continued to be used into the 20th century, and they are now museums.

Another Asian country that was much influenced by Europe during the 19th century was India. Trading companies from both England and France had established outposts in India in the 17th century. When the British defeated the French at Plassey, northeastern India, in 1757, they began a two-century-long rule of the Indian subcontinent, and the British East India Company enjoyed a virtual monopoly on trade in that region. Following the Indian Mutiny (1857–1859), most of the country came under the direct rule of the British government. Areas that were not under British control were protected by native hereditary rulers, who exercised various degrees of autonomy. There was a substantial British population in India, and many of the native rulers, following the Turkish example, chose to build palaces that were, at least in part, based on Western styles. The opening of the Suez Canal in 1869 facilitated both shipping and travel between England and India. Europeans desired Indian fabrics and other goods, and large quantities of English and French furniture, lighting fixtures, and glassware were exported to India.

Most of the Indian rulers were extremely wealthy, and they usually displayed their wealth in the form of luxurious palaces and furnishings. The older palaces were often decorated with inlaid walls that sparkled with colored glass and mirrored inserts. A room ornamented in this style was known as a "Sheesh Mahal" (Figs. 2-10 and 2-11),[5] and it was frequently found in the women's quarters. From the mid-18th century, English and French glass chandeliers were popular fixtures, and some palaces were decorated with European-made

FIGURE 2-10

Mirrored walls in the Sheesh Mahal (Palace of Mirrors), Motibagh Palace, Patiala, India, 18th century.

FIGURE 2-11

Mirrored walls and ceiling in the Sheesh Mahal, City Palace, Udaipur, India, 18th century.

FIGURE 2-12

Glass finials on the City
Palace, Udaipur. Probably
English, 19th century.

glass finials as well (Fig. 2-12). It was probably this love of color and sparkle that later prompted the Indian rulers to embrace the idea of colored glass chandeliers and glass furniture—a taste that was not shared in Europe. Furniture made of glass or silver was especially popular in India, since it did not deteriorate in the hot and muggy climate, as Western wooden furniture did.

With the exception of Rajasthan in northwestern India, the princely states did not have lavishly furnished palaces before the late 19th century. Furniture in the Western sense—tables, chairs, and beds—was not used there. Instead, the residents sat and slept on floor cushions and mats. The only necessary article of furniture was a chest for storage. However, as the British extended their influence, the Indians sought European tutors and foreign travel for heirs to the throne, and the nation's wealthy princes began to adopt Western ways and to build Western-style palaces.

FIGURE 2-13

Detail of mirrored wall in the Sheesh Mahal, Motibagh Palace.

FIGURE 2-14

Exterior of durbar hall, Qila Mubarak, Patiala.

FIGURE 2-15

Portrait of the maharajah Mohinder Singh
(r. 1862–1876), Motibagh Palace.

Some princes hired European architects, while others
employed British army engineers. Most of these palaces combined classical or Italianate architecture with
elements of Indian design. Both of these styles used
domes and colonnades, as well as clusters of arches.[6]

The Motibagh Palace, located at Patiala in the Punjab, northwestern India, was one of the largest of these
palaces. Built by the maharajah Nerindera Singh (r.
1845–1862) in the 1850s, it is said to have been one of
the grandest private residences in Asia (Fig. 2-13). The
Qila Mubarak (fort) had been the royal residence before that time. Its durbar[7] hall (Fig. 2-14) has a collection of more than 20 Osler chandeliers purchased by
Mohinder Singh (r. 1862–1876; Fig. 2-15) in the 1870s
(Fig. 2-16).

Figure 2-16

Durbar hall of the Qila Mubarak (fort), adjacent to the Motibagh Palace, with several Osler chandeliers made in the 1870s.

FIGURE 2-17

Jai Vilas Palace, Gwalior, India. It was built in the early 1870s in anticipation of a visit from the Prince of Wales.

Gwalior's Jai Vilas Palace (Fig. 2-17) was constructed by Jayaji Rao Scindia, one of India's richest rulers, in the early 1870s. It was built in anticipation of a visit to India from the Prince of Wales, which lasted from November 1875 to January 1876. The palace's durbar hall includes two of the largest chandeliers constructed by Osler (Fig. 2-18). Each of them is more than 40 feet in height. According to palace records,

elephants were hoisted onto the roof to make sure that it could support the weight of these colossal chandeliers. Another outstanding feature of this palace is the banisters on the staircase that ascends to the durbar hall (Fig. 2-19). A particularly Indian feature is a swing that is heavily decorated with glass, including prisms from broken chandeliers (Fig. 2-20).

European Glass Furnishings for Eastern Palaces

FIGURE 2-18

Interior of the durbar hall, Jai Vilas Palace. It features mammoth Osler chandeliers and some glass torchères and small glass tables.

FIGURE 2-19

Staircase ascending to the durbar hall, Jai Vilas Palace. In addition to glass banisters, the foyer contains a red chandelier and candelabra made by Osler.

FIGURE 2-20

Glass swing in the Jai Vilas Palace. The swing was made locally, and many of the glass parts are chandelier prisms.

FIGURE 2-21

The City Palace in Udaipur, northwestern India, was started in the 17th century, and it is now a complex that includes buildings added in the 18th and 19th centuries (Fig. 2-21). It houses the largest known collection of glass furniture (Figs. 2-22 and 2-23). Most of these pieces were made by Osler, and they were acquired by Maharana[8] Sajjan Singh (r. 1874–1884) between 1878 and 1882 and by his successor, Maharana Fateh Singh (r. 1884–1930), until the 1920s. During this time, the maharanas bought two settees, a bed, numerous tables and chairs, a small fountain, lamps, a shrine, and other pieces that were used in a variety of locations within the City Palace complex. Some of the later purchases were never unpacked because they ar-

FIGURE 2-21

City Palace, Udaipur, India. This complex, consisting of several palaces, was built over three centuries.

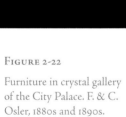

FIGURE 2-22

Furniture in crystal gallery
of the City Palace. F. & C.
Osler, 1880s and 1890s.

FIGURE 2-23

Cut glass bed in the City
Palace. F. & C. Osler, 1890s.

rived after Fateh Singh's death. However, the present maharana has gathered all of these pieces together in a crystal gallery in the durbar hall, where they make a stunning display.

The palace also features some of the most elaborate mirrored inlay work in India, as well as colored glass windows (Fig. 2-24). It includes a chair inlaid with glass (Fig. 2-25) that fits the style of the palace's Sheesh Mahal.

The Faluknuma and Chowmalla Palaces in Hyderabad, southern India, also have large quantities of English glass chandeliers and candelabra, as well as some examples of French and Bohemian glass. The former palace was constructed in 1872 and purchased by the nizam (ruler) in 1897. The palaces at Jaipur, Jodhpur, Baroda, and Bikaner each contain chandeliers and a few pieces of glass furniture, mostly tables and chairs, and there are some examples in other palaces as well. Most of the royal families purchased this furniture in small quantities. The rulers of Patiala, Gwalior, and Udaipur were the principal buyers of both chandeliers and glass furniture, and many examples are still on display in their palaces.

Figure 2-24

Colored glass window in the City Palace, 19th century.

Figure 2-25

Wooden chair with glass inlays in the City Palace, 19th century.

Not all of this glass was delivered exclusively to palaces, however. The maharajahs were certainly the leaders in terms of taste and fashion, but they were not the only customers for imported wares. Prosperous civil servants, both British and Indian, patronized stores in Delhi, Bombay, and Calcutta that were stocked with European china and glassware.

Most of the lighting devices and all of the furniture and fountains were made by the firms that are discussed in the following chapters. Some other English manufacturers supplied chandeliers to India. As early as 1790, John Blades of London was supplying cut glass lighting fixtures and tableware to India and the Near East. He is said to have made a mausoleum of emerald green glass that was 14 feet high for the nabob of Oude in 1795, as well as cut glass tables for the ruler of Egypt. The shah of Persia and the nizam of Hyderabad were also customers, but no illustrations of these commissions survive.[9] At least two examples marked by Henry Greene, also a London maker, were in the Chowmalla Palace in Hyderabad,[10] and there are probably others still in India. A. S. Nash, yet another London glassmaker, is known to have provided lighting fixtures to India. Some recent publications on the palaces[11] have maintained that most of this glass furniture was made in Belgium, but there is no indication that the Cristalleries de Val St. Lambert, the largest Belgian glass factory in the late 19th century, or any other Belgian firm, made any of these pieces. A small number of these chandeliers seem to have originated in Venice and Bohemia, but the great majority are English and French, and they can be reliably attributed to specific factories.

Only a few of these objects have survived. Nevertheless, they have become popular in Europe and the United States, where examples can occasionally be found in antique shops and auction houses. These pieces were made at a specific time and for a limited market. They are fantastic examples of what the marriage of design and technology can achieve. We are fortunate that their owners cherished and preserved them. With the information on the manufacturers of these objects that is presented in the following chapters, perhaps more of them can be identified.

F. & C. Osler

FIGURE 3-1

Candelabrum, one of a pair created by F. & C. Osler for the tomb of Muhammad at Medina, 1847. From Smith [note 1].

F. & C. OSLER was probably the largest European company that supplied glass objects to India. Its products sold there included both table wares and lighting devices. During the last quarter of the 1800s and the early years of the following century, Osler also made glass fountains and furniture for the Indian market.

The Osler firm was founded in Birmingham, England, in 1807. Thomas Osler and a partner produced small ornaments, followed by glass prisms and parts for chandeliers. In 1831, Osler's sons, Follett and Clarkson, assumed control of the business, which was eventually reorganized as F. & C. Osler. They moved to new premises in Birmingham, and in 1852 they opened their own glass factory so that they no longer had to rely on others for their glass. As early as 1840, the Oslers associated themselves with a silver and jewelry house in Calcutta and began to display their chandeliers and wall brackets there. By November 1843, they had hired their own agent in Calcutta, and shortly thereafter, they opened a store at Dalhousie Square, which eventually sold glassware of all kinds as well as lighting devices. In 1845, they opened a London showroom at 44 Oxford Street, and they maintained both of these facilities into the 20th century. It seems somewhat surprising that the Oslers had a showroom in India before they had one in London, but this underscores the fact that they were targeting the market in India before any of the other English glass companies.

In the late 1840s, the Oslers capitalized on visits to Birmingham of several heads of state to advertise their ability to make lighting devices on a scale that had not previously been attempted. This effort began with a pair of "colossal candelabra" (Fig. 3-1)[1] that were ordered in

1847 for the tomb of Muhammad at Medina by Ibrahim Pasha (1789–1848), an Egyptian general and heir to the throne. Standing 17 feet tall, the candelabra were probably the largest such lighting devices ever produced, and there was a considerable amount of publicity about them. "The pillars are constructed to carry twenty-four lights each, and as we have intimated, are composed entirely of pure crystal glass, cut in a style the richest and most chaste, . . ." *The Art-Union* reported. "The column itself is composed of three cylinders, of cut glass prisms.... The total weight of one candelabrum is nearly 2,000 lbs."[2] This order, and subsequent ones for Queen Victoria and the palace of the ruler of Nepal, prompted Follett Osler to propose a "Central Fountain of Crystal Glass and of proportional size" to the committee that was then organizing London's Great Exhibition of 1851, and the offer was accepted.[3]

Osler's Crystal Fountain was probably the most spectacular display at this exhibition, the first world's fair (Fig. 3-2). It stood in the center of the Crystal Palace, was 27 feet tall, and is said to have required four tons of glass to construct it. It was destroyed when the glass building burned in the 1930s, but there are several prints showing how it was installed. The *Art-Journal*'s reporter described it as "perhaps the most striking object in the Exhibition; the lightness and beauty, as well as the perfect novelty of its design, have rendered it the theme of admiration with all visitors. The ingenuity with which this has been effected is very perfect; it is supported by bars of iron, which are so completely embedded in the glass shafts, as to be invisible, and in no degree interfering with the purity and crystalline effect of the whole object."[4] The iron piping and supports were cleverly hidden by molded and cut glass pieces, and the effect was truly dazzling. The fountain was characterized as "an object which, of all others, is calculated to disarm criticism, and put an end to cavilling upon matters aesthetic. The purity of the material, the brilliancy of the cutting, the tasteful arrangement, the appropriate selection of form, all indicate the presence of correct taste and cunning hands . . . its gem-like surface and cuttings turning everything by its prismatic influence into purple and emerald and gold. . . ."[5] This was the first (and probably the largest) of several cut and molded glass fountains that Osler and other glasshouses created in the second half of the 19th century.

Osler's other notable display at the Crystal Palace exhibition was a pair of eight-foot candelabra that had been purchased by Prince Albert for Queen Victoria in 1848 (Fig. 3-3). These objects held 15 candles each, and they can still be seen today at Osborne House on the Isle of Wight. Osler registered a similar design on November 22, 1849 (Fig. 3-4), but, as noted above, it had been creating such large lighting devices since 1847. A 20-foot fixture was ordered for the royal palace of Nepal in 1849.[6]

Because of its reflective qualities, the colorless cut glass for which the English glass industry was famous was particularly suitable for large lighting devices. During the next several decades, Osler's basic design was repeated, with variations and in ever increasing sizes, for many customers. It is probably not surprising that the firm's most important early customers were from Asia, since the English taste in interior decoration favored simpler products in the 1840s. The extensive publicity engendered by these orders, which were featured in such magazines as *The Art-Union*, must have greatly increased the demand for such fixtures. It also helped to make these products

FIGURE 3-2

Print showing Osler's Crystal Fountain in the center of the Crystal Palace, 1851. From M. Digby Wyatt, *The Industrial Arts of the Nineteenth Century*, London: Day and Son, 1851–1853, v. 1, pl. 23. Juliette K. and Leonard S. Rakow Research Library of The Corning Museum of Glass, Corning, New York.

PLATE 23

W. DIXON WRGTT. DIRECT.   E. CLOPORU DEL ET LITH.

F. & C. OSLER   53

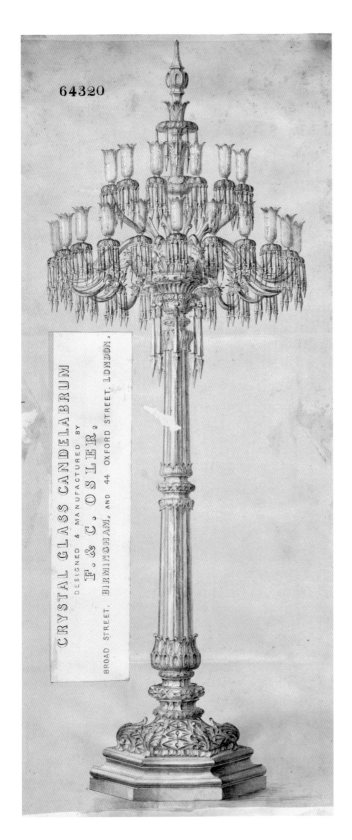

64320

CRYSTAL GLASS CANDELABRUM
DESIGNED & MANUFACTURED BY
F. & C. OSLER,
BROAD STREET, BIRMINGHAM, AND 44 OXFORD STREET, LONDON.

FIGURE 3-4

Design for Osler candela-
brum, registered November
22, 1849. The National Archives U.K. (TNA(PRO)
BT43/60 64320).

a specialty for the Birmingham company, which had
focused on the production of chandeliers before that
time.

It was undoubtedly the success of the Crystal Fountain and other large pieces that led the Osler brothers
to open their own glasshouse in Birmingham in 1852.
The use of gas for lighting was gradually increasing in
England at that time, especially in public buildings and
among the wealthy. Osler, like Defries, made fixtures
for gas, candle, colza oil, and, after 1860, kerosene devices.[7]

The Osler firm continued to display its large and
impressive designs at subsequent world's fairs. A 30-
foot gas candelabrum shown at the Paris exposition
of 1855 was praised by Georges Bontemps, a glass ex-
pert. "Mess'rs. Osler seem to have attained perfection:
general beauty of form, boldness of adjustment, purity,
whiteness, and brilliancy," he wrote.[8] The design of this
candelabrum was somewhat different from that of earlier examples, especially at the base, which displayed
more decoration than fixtures made in the 1840s.

At the second London world's fair, held in 1862, Osler erected a tall, narrow glass case to hold its exhibit.
Designed by the noted architect Owen Jones, the case
featured engraved glass panels at the top and a radiat-
ing star gasolier by which it was lighted (Fig. 3-5). Osler also displayed a pair of 20-foot gas fixtures (Fig. 3-6),
which, judging from the illustration in the exhibition
catalog, were virtually identical to the taller fixture that
had previously been shown in Paris.

Fortunately for researchers, some Osler archival materials are housed in the Birmingham Museum and Art
Gallery and the Birmingham City Library, and they
provide information about the firm's customers and
the Indian trade. In addition, there are two large pattern books with hand-drawn and colored designs that
are numbered and usually dated, although customers

are rarely named. The Osler company certainly had plenty of customers in England, but it also managed a very large export business. As early as October 5, 1862, it supplied a 24-light green chandelier, with two tiers of candles, to J. G. Garrett & Company, and in February and September 1863, one of the design books shows 40-light purple and 24-light "ruby plated" chandeliers made for the same customer. As previously noted (see page 20), one critic at the 1862 world's fair in London had written that colored chandeliers were a design mistake, so it is likely that Garrett shipped these chandeliers to the East. The pattern book records a number of designs for colored

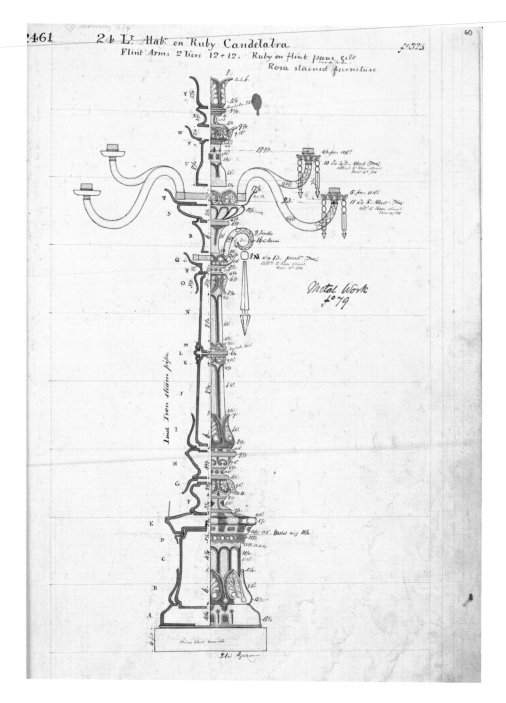

chandeliers and candelabra in the 1860s and 1870s (Fig. 3-7), as well as for some fixtures with colorless parts. There were also designs with "colored furniture" (Fig. 3-8), which refers to beads and prisms. Some of the fixtures were plated, or made with two layers of glass (Fig. 3-9). The top layer, which was often white, was cut through to reveal the colored glass beneath it. White on ruby was the most popular combination, although alabaster on green was also frequently employed. These plated fixtures were

FIGURE 3-7

Design for candelabrum, 1860s, from Osler pattern book, v. 1, p. 60. Birmingham Museum and Art Gallery, Birmingham.

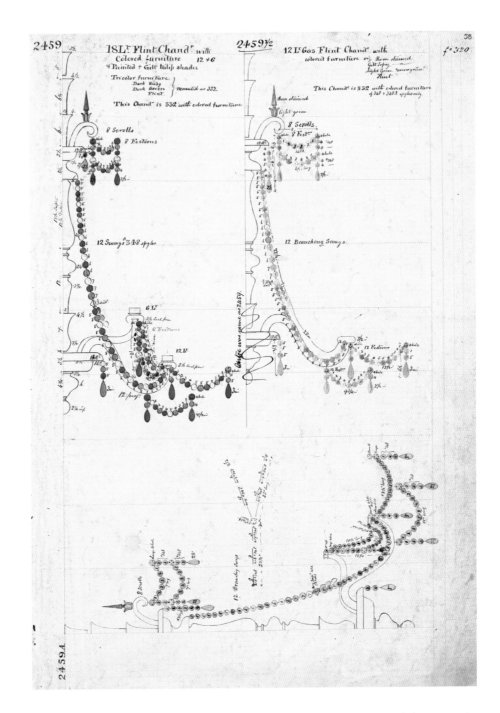

often gilded (Fig. 3-10). In the design books, most of them are shown with tulip shades, although the shades were usually purchased separately.

Such a variety of offerings was not always received enthusiastically. A letter from the manager of the Calcutta store to the head office, dated September 24, 1857, maintains that "fancy and coloured chandeliers are bad stock. . . . It will be always well to keep a few coloured ones but let them be of one plain colour and *all glass*, say red and

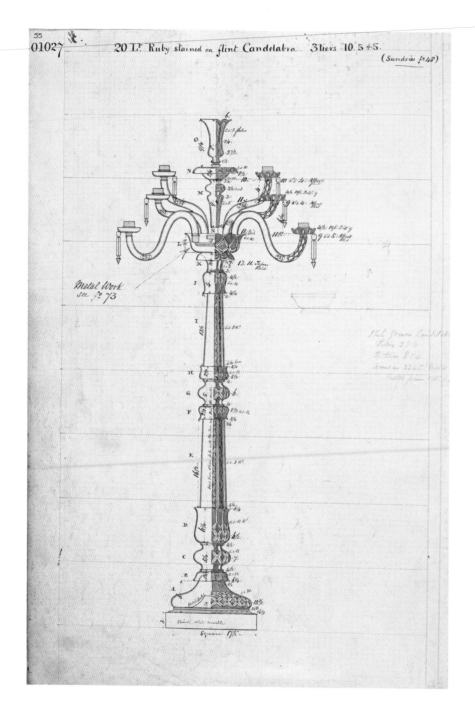

FIGURE 3-9

Design for candelabrum, 1860s, from Osler pattern book, v. 1, p. 55. Birmingham Museum and Art Gallery, Birmingham.

green as the colours. . . . But I think we can never expect a quick sale for any coloured chandeliers our experience proves the force of this."[9] Despite this pessimistic outlook, colored chandeliers sold very well for the next half-century, as is demonstrated in letters sent from the Calcutta office to Birmingham.

The surviving letters describing Osler's business in India date from the 1840s to the 1870s, so they do not include the later furniture orders. Nevertheless, it is evident

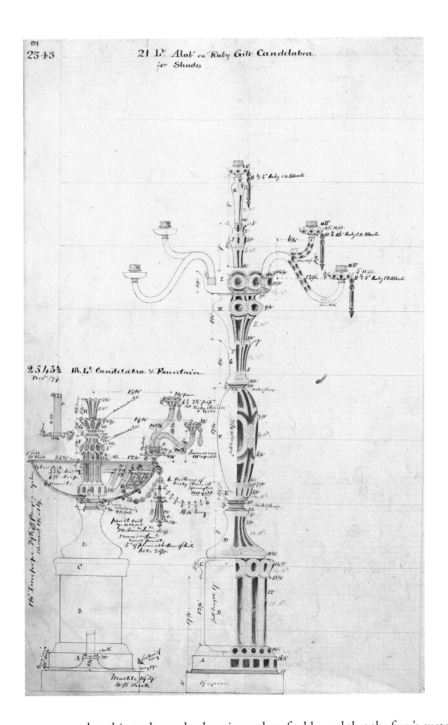

that this trade was both active and profitable, and that the firm's customers included
several royal families. A letter of May 29, 1858, states that "the Rajah of Serampore
has sent his salaam[10] with an intimation that he purposed visiting us tomorrow. . . .
Our old friend the Puttiala [i.e., Patiala] Rajah has been a strong and valuable ally to
us. . . . He is a noble fellow. . . . We shall write him when the road is open as a re-
minder that we are still here and no doubt something will come of it."[11] At that time,

the "Puttiala Rajah" was Nerindera Singh (r. 1845–1862), who rebuilt the Qila Mubarak and the Motibagh Palace, located in Patiala in the Punjab, northwestern India, in the 1840s and 1850s. Both of these buildings include quantities of colored and colorless chandeliers, most of which were made by Osler (Figs. 3-11 and 3-12). Nerindera Singh had fought for the British during the Indian Mutiny (1857–1859), which is why the letter refers to him as a "noble fellow."

On February 9, 1869, the Calcutta store reported, "The Temple is set up in the back room and is now being touched up a little to make it look fresh, but it does not require so much doing as was thought necessary."[12] Unfortunately, there is no picture of this structure, so unlike the example made by Defries that is discussed on page 100, we can only guess at its appearance and size. Later communications that year reported that "I hear the Gwalior Rajah has a new palace to furnish. If so, we will no doubt come in for a share—at present it is only rumor . . ." (June 25) and "it is cheering to be able to report sales of . . . chandeliers. We have opened and set up some of the new coloured chandeliers, red, blue, green, opal and gilt. They are very handsome indeed, but I would not recommend too much of that sort of stock. I shall be anxious to get rid of it as soon as possible for more than the usual reasons. There seems a great opening for chandeliers at Puttiala and I shall not neglect to keep my eye on that bright spot . . ." (October 20). The Osler store in Calcutta was also trying to attract more customers from the Indian middle class. The opportunities at Patia-

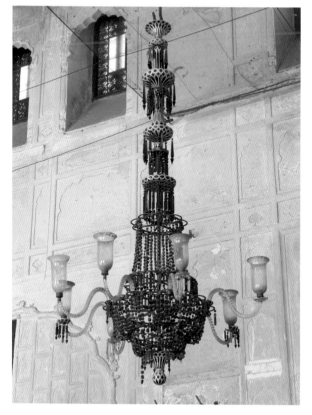

FIGURE 3-13

Table lamp in the Sheesh
Mahal at Motibagh Palace,
Patiala. Probably F. & C.
Osler, 1870s.

FIGURE 3-14

Candelabrum, one of a pair,
in the Sheesh Mahal at Motibagh Palace, Patiala. Probably
F. & C. Osler, 1870s.

la resulted from the presence there of a new ruler, Mohinder Singh (r. 1862–1876),
who had inherited the title and was refurbishing the palace.

A price list dated October 6, 1868, shows the prices and sizes of lighting devices
that were ordered by Mohinder Singh for Patiala. These were probably candelabra,
rather than chandeliers.

Pair 7 Lt.	Green cased	01102	34£	
7 Lt.	Ruby cased	01102	36	
6 Lt.	Ruby	2396	21	
6 Lt.	Ruby cased	2527	19	
8 Lt.	Ruby cased	2527	24	
12 Lt.	Ruby cased	2527	37	
5 plain green shades	@ 3/	2£ 5'		
22 plain ruby shades	@ 7/	£ 7/12		
28 Gilt line ruby shades	@ 8/	£ 11/4		
9 Lge flint shades		£ 2-/-6		
Duty		16/12/11[13]		

The goods plus the tax cost £211, and the Patiala government apparently paid for this
shipment. Some of the lighting fixtures that can be seen in the palace today were probably part of this order (Figs. 3-13 and 3-14).

A letter of November 3, 1868, mentions "a considerable demand for ornamental lighting" and says that the writer wants to install gas for lighting in the shop. He also mentions a very large Osler chandelier that had just been installed in the Calcutta opera house, adding that "Calcutta has never seen anything like it."[14]

On November 16, 1868, the writer reported a second trip to Patiala and sales of £311 on October 31, stating that these were "not as profitable as the first sale but it has led to the Raja promising us a good order so soon as the new palace is finished. We sent up a large candelabrum [Fig. 3-15] for his inspection."

In January and February 1869, the store reported good sales, but the manager was doubtful about future sales of colored pieces. However, on February 23, he stated that "4 of the Blue & gold 8 Lt. Chandeliers are gone off. I would not advocate their being replaced as they are too costly...." On July 1, he wrote: "Regarding the chandelier of 24 Lights, No. 2546 in Oxford St..., it appears to me to be the very thing required for the Puttiala Raja, but a few changes are necessary.... The pattern is very rich indeed. Have you been able to give any attention to the design for the fountain?"

Subsequent letters mention that "the Maharaja of Scindia arrived yesterday" (December 27, 1869) and "the Scindia Raja who purchased the [illegible] temple, 2 candelabra of 50 Lt and 40 Lt." This is probably a reference to the maharajah of Gwalior, a member of the Scindia family. The Gwalior palace has a number of Osler chandeliers, as well as a fountain, and Gwalior and Patiala are the two palaces that seem to be most often mentioned in these letters. Another notable visitor to the Osler shop in India was Prince Alfred, duke of Edinburgh and a son of Queen Victoria, who arrived on December 29, 1869. A letter of January 4, 1870, says that sales during the last month of 1869 were "the best we ever had."

On March 8, 1870, the writer reported that he had "received your letter about the large fountain, 8,000 rupees delivered in Puttiala. Price so large makes it doubtful we will get the order.... All the chandeliers are suspended at Puttiala and the candelabrum placed in the receptions room...." This letter also mentions inexpensive imported chandeliers at Patiala, but it adds that the maharajah had promised to buy only from Osler in the future. "The Puttiala Raja has been a minor until recently... now that he has come of age, he is spending prodigiously," the writer added. The invoice for the Patiala chandelier order includes four ruby, two green, two amber, and eight flint examples, the colored ones in two sizes and the flint ones in several sizes, with all of them including shades, for a total price of £1,345/10/6 or 30,340 rupees.

Although the writer of the letters was consistently pessimistic about costs and future orders, Mohinder Singh did purchase the fountain (Fig. 3-16), which was installed outside the palace. It had been displayed in Osler's London showroom, where it was described as follows:

> A platform of richly-cut glass rests upon a white marble-base, from which rises a massive central shaft, surrounded by six smaller columns composed of prisms, also richly cut.... An elegant foliated neckpiece... serves to support a capacious basin of crystal, eight feet in diameter. This basin is deeply escal-

FIGURE 3-15

Candelabrum in durbar hall at Qila Mubarak, Patiala. F. & C. Osler, 1870s.

FIGURE 3-16

Osler glass fountain in the Sheesh Mahal at Motibagh Palace, Patiala. It was originally installed in the palace gardens in 1874.

loped, and cut on the under side to represent the ripple and play of water, which it does very effectively. . . . The total height of this magnificent fountain is twenty-three feet six inches, and its weight, exclusive of the marble base, is two and a quarter tons. Its elegant proportions, originality, and beauty of design, combined with perfection of workmanship . . . have certainly not been surpassed, even if equalled, by anything of the kind we remember to have seen. The fountain has been sent to India for the palace of his Highness the Maharajah of Puttiala, . . . who purchased it."[15]

Today, the fountain is installed inside the Motibagh Palace, where it can be viewed by the public, but without water. The "basin" mentioned by the writer is a design feature that is also found in many of the Osler chandeliers. In the fountain that was later purchased for Gwalior, the basin was reversed and used to protect the electric lights from the water (Fig. 3-17).

Correspondence from Osler's Calcutta store to the Birmingham home office also includes entries stating that

+ The writer is "glad to know about Mr. Nell. We hear about him from Puttiala and are satisfied he has bought largely from Defries" (June 11, 1870). Apparently, Nell had tried unsuccessfully to sell wares to Patiala.

+ "The Puttiala Raja is desirous of having some glass mantel pieces and asks for a design. Please send 2 or 3 suitable for large rooms" (March 21, 1873). Although the Osler pattern book contains drawings of these objects, they do not seem to have been purchased.

+ "Mr. Elsworth has gone to Cashmere [Kashmir] to try the temper of the Maharajah who is much more wealthy than any Ruler in that part of the world and is said to have a great weakness for glass" (September 3, 1870). The writer also noted that the Patiala ruler was annoyed that he had been waiting for two years to take delivery of a 112-light chandelier. On September 28, 1870, Elsworth was respectfully received at Gwalior and promised an order of a fountain that had originally been suggested by the Defries firm, which offered to make two of them. The following November, the writer was going to Baroda, a city in Rajasthan, northwestern India, to see the gaekwar (ruler) there. In January 1871, Elsworth reported that Defries had an agent in Bombay, the firm of J. Watson & Sons, but added that "there is not much business in Bombay."

A letter of January 20, 1875, reports an order totaling £10,000 or £20,000 from an agent of a "native prince," who requested drawings of chandeliers and candelabra.

FIGURE 3-17

Glass fountain with electric lights and glass balustrade in the Jai Vilas Palace, Gwalior. F. & C. Osler, probably about 1899.

Enclosed with this correspondence were two other letters, one of which was an estimate, dated July 28, 1874, that Defries apparently gave the maharajah; the other was signed by A. S. Nash, a London glassmaker. The "native prince" was identified as the maharajah of Gwalior, and the proposals were for the fittings of the durbar hall, part of the Jai Vilas Palace, which was then under construction. Defries's proposal included several huge gas or candle fixtures for a sum of £2,403, as well as wooden furniture and an iron stair railing. However, the order was eventually placed with Osler, although there are few details in the surviving correspondence.

The durbar hall, which was constructed in 1872–1874 for a visit from the Prince of Wales that occurred in 1875–1876, holds two huge Osler chandeliers. The foyer contains a chandelier (Fig. 3-18), a glass balustrade (Fig. 3-19a), and two multi-branched candelabra (Fig. 3-20a). The Osler pattern book includes designs for the balustrade

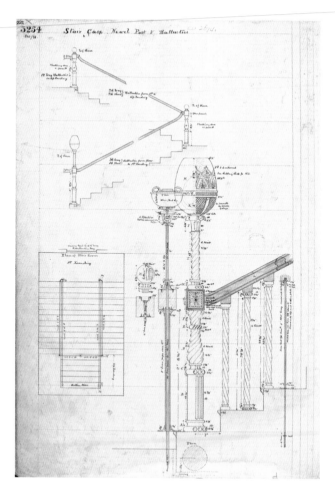

and the candelabra (Figs. 3-19b and 3-20b). The palace was built in Western style with classical and Italianate features, and its chandeliers are also European in style. They weigh several tons apiece.

In 1878, the production of large glass objects took another leap forward when the Osler, Baccarat, and Pantin firms displayed glass furniture at the Exposition Universelle in Paris. One reporter, commenting on the artistry and beauty of Osler's mammoth chandeliers, noted: "The prismatic colours blended like rainbow hues from every point of this enormous structure, and made it a point of predominant attraction to visitors. It was more fitted for the throne-room of some magnificent Eastern despot than for anything else."[16] Another writer stated that "considerable amusement is experienced by French [v]isitors and foreigners at finding crystal used for chairs and sofas—probably furniture intended for the proverbial glass house."[17] A later issue of the same publication described these pieces more fully:

> There is a splendid crystal chair of state and footstool. The framework is of cut glass, arranged in skilfully devised patterns, glittering like a mass of gems, which will attract the notice of many of the Eastern potentates who visit the Exhibition. At the back of the court is a cabinet, which is a truly magnificent

FIGURE 3-19A

Glass balustrade in foyer of the durbar hall at Jai Vilas Palace, Gwalior. F. & C. Osler, 1875.

FIGURE 3-19B

Design for balustrade shown in Figure 3-19a, 1870s, from Osler pattern book, v. 1, p. 221. Birmingham Museum and Art Gallery, Birmingham.

piece of workmanship of pure Gothic design. The back, which is formed by a large pier glass [mirror], is without spot or blemish. The body of the cabinet, composed of cut glass pillars and panels, is one mass of engraving and cutting. Although a very large number of pieces have been used, the nicety with which they are joined is such that the keenest eye is unable to detect the points of union; while the refined taste with which this cabinet is executed is worthy of the old masters. . . . The combination of the darkened woodwork, ormolu work, and gilt carvings make up a whole, which for beauty of design and boldness of execution is unsurpassed, and will do not a little to enhance the reputation already gained by Messrs. Osler for their manufacture of glass.[18]

Another critic offered the following observations:

The glass chair, too, with its rich silk velvet seat and its marvelous prismatic colours, suggested powerfully the idea of the old Moorish Alhambra; ideas of Persian splendour were more than realized in these gorgeous objects. Glass chiffonier, glass chairs, glass tables, and, above all, glass pillars, on which stood

FIGURE 3-20A

Multi-branched candelabrum in case at Jai Vilas Palace, Gwalior. F. & C. Osler, 1875.

FIGURE 3-20B

Design for candelabrum shown in Figure 3-20a, 1870s, from Osler pattern book, v. 1, p. 62. Birmingham Museum and Art Gallery, Birmingham.

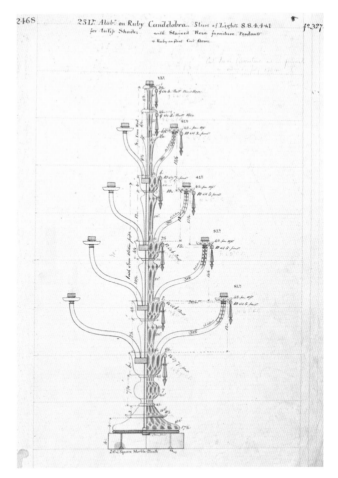

glass candelabra of the purest lustre and the most severe simplicity, combined to make this part of the British Section as attractive as any in the building. Whether chairs and tables are a proper direction for glass manufacture I leave others to decide. However much sound judgement may condemn such a course, I confess to having been really dazzled by this display; all was so simple, pure, chaste, and elegant that misapplication of material was atoned for by the rich full colour of the mass. . . .[19]

These objects were shown in the Furniture Court, rather than with the rest of the glass. One writer reported that "this cabinet and an arm chair and stool . . . are not likely to find purchasers in England, but are more suited, and I hear are intended, to adorn the palace of some Eastern Potentate."[20] An American publication described the chair as covered with rich crimson velvet and glittering like a mass of gems.[21] Osler also exhibited a number of large chandeliers and candelabra at the Paris exposition. They represented a technical breakthrough in that, although the cabinet, chair, and stool, like the chandeliers, were assembled from many smaller pieces of glass, they were very thick pieces, and the ability to anneal something such as a chair leg was relatively new. Not all of the critics admired these objects, however. One writer stated: "It may be a triumph of mechanical skill to produce a throne or a buffet in solid glass, but surely utterly inconsistent with the real use of the material; and while it is legitimate to employ the highest talent, . . . surely it is utterly out of keeping with the real purpose of the material, which is at once brittle and risky to move without extreme care, to employ it for furniture stands and other works of the kind."[22]

Although Osler's glass furniture was admired by the public, it did not win any awards, and this was to be the last world's fair that featured glass made by the firm. The cabinet was illustrated in the catalog of the exposition (Fig. 3-21),[23] but there was very little description, and the piece has since disappeared. The chair and stool were not illustrated, although the catalog contained pictures of a chandelier and a relatively simple candelabrum, both made of colorless glass.[24] Osler made another cabinet (Fig. 3-22), which was subsequently sold to an Eastern buyer. This object is now in a private American collection. Its design in the company's pattern books is dated May 1887, and it is unlikely that more than one example was made. However, those books contain more than one design for chairs, and several of them seem to have been produced.

A lengthy article on the Osler firm and its showrooms in Dalhousie Square, Calcutta, appeared in an Indian publication in late 1883. It mentioned the Great Central Fountain, which stood in a pool of water 12

FIGURE 3-21

Gothic-style glass cabinet exhibited by Osler at the 1878 world's fair in Paris. From *The Illustrated Catalogue of the Paris International Exhibition, 1878* [note 23]. Juliette K. and Leonard S. Rakow Research Library of The Corning Museum of Glass, Corning, New York.

FIGURE 3-22

Glass cabinet. F. & C. Osler, about 1887 (design no. 2996). H. 307 cm, W. 193 cm. Private collection.

feet across and was surrounded by a glass balustrade 11 feet tall. "When the fountain is working, the eye is agreeably deceived, and it is difficult to tell where the water ends and the glass begins," the article noted, adding:

> Let me speak of the bedsteads, the Ottoman, the sofa and chairs of glass. Here they are. Let the world come and see them. They show us the possibilities of glass manufacture in a way that no treatise and no illustration could.

The bedstead is 7 feet 6 inches by 4 feet 6 inches. The framework of it is of brass, and malleable iron, but neither brass nor iron are visible. Except the upholstery of crimson velvet, nothing is seen but massive cut glass. . . . The Ottoman and the sofas are very similar as to the glass construction, and exactly similar to the bed in upholstery. Indeed, I am informed that they have been disposed of to a native prince; and therefore, I apprehend, will form the furniture *en suite* of an apartment. . . . The coolness of appearance will certainly be a great recommendation in a climate like that of India.[25]

The article also described "corner whatnots," tables (Fig. 3-23), mirrors with glass frames, a clock in a crystal case, tables of blue glass ("which though of itself less beautiful to the eye, is certainly a relief to the large amount of crystal around it"), chandeliers for kerosene and for candles, and a model of a Moorish temple in which fish bowls and a small crystal fountain were placed. Glass hookahs (Fig. 3-24)[26] and dinner services consisting of a *thala* (rice dish) and cups for chutney[27] and ghee (clarified butter) were also a specialty of Osler's Indian shop.

The furniture described in this chapter was quite popular with the Indian public, and it was especially favored by princely families. An example of a blue glass table (Fig. 3-25) has been found, and although the design does not appear in either of

FIGURE 3-23

Small glass table with prisms encircling a velvet-covered rim. This table may be similar to those shown in Calcutta in 1883.

FIGURE 3-24

Hookah and *bajot* (small table) in crystal gallery of City Palace, Udaipur. F. & C. Osler, probably 1880s.

Figure 3-25

Blue glass table, blown, cut;
assembled on metal shaft
marked "F. and C. Osler,"
1880–1885. OH. 75.0 cm,
Diam. (max.) 43.6 cm. The
Corning Museum of Glass,
Corning, New York
(2005.2.11).

FIGURE 3-26

Design (no. 2537) for red and white chandelier, from Osler catalog, 1883. Birmingham Museum and Art Gallery, Birmingham.

FIGURE 3-27

Three fountains shown in Osler catalog, 1883. Birmingham Museum and Art Gallery, Birmingham.

the pattern books, the metal fittings of the object are marked "F. & C. Osler." Several identical tables are known in colorless glass, so the design was apparently well received. As far as we are aware, this is the first colored glass table to come to light.

Osler published several catalogs that are useful for documenting the company's production, but furniture appears only in the catalogs distributed in India. An armchair and a side chair are shown in a catalog published about 1880, and another catalog, dated three years later, has red and white (Fig. 3-26), green and white, blue and white, and gold-colored chandeliers, as well as several fountains (Fig. 3-27), table lamps, and centerpieces. The 1894 catalog, which shows the firm's new address at 12 Old Courthouse Street, Calcutta, includes mainly tableware and smaller chandeliers, and it has no furniture. However, furniture could still be ordered at that time, judging from the dates in the design books.

The first of the two Osler pattern books, now in the Birmingham Museum and Art Gallery, is dated 1874 on the second page, but it contains some colored chandelier designs that are dated 1862 and 1863 on pages 41–43. A green chandelier (Fig. 3-28) on page 251, near the end of the book, is dated November 1896.[28] Most of the earliest designs, which are from the 1860s and 1870s, are for colored chandeliers and candelabra. These are clearly candle fixtures, and most of them are illustrated with matching colored tulip shades with gilded decoration (Fig. 3-29). Another standing fixture, dated July 1884, is also shown, and two examples are found in the durbar hall of the Jai Vilas Palace in Gwalior (see Figure 3-20a, b). The design for Gwalior's glass staircase was made in that same year (see Figure 3-19a, b), but the piece was ordered again in October 1891.

A 12-foot-tall fountain with a downward-arching basin bears the pencil notation "Bahawalpur, 1878," and it was reordered with electric lights in October 1899. A similar fountain with the basin inverted is dated May 1883 in the design book. It seems that only some of the fountains that Osler supplied have survived.

There are several designs for chairs, settees, beds, and tables, and each of them appears to have been manufactured and sent to India for a particular buyer, even though it may have been reordered by someone else. Therefore, the designs are not necessarily unique, and a few of them may have been made on speculation.

The first of the furniture designs is for a chair with a back of embossed (i.e., acid-etched) silvered glass and a matching footstool (Figs. 3-30 and 3-31), and it seems to date from 1875 or 1876. The next design (Fig. 3-32a), which is dated December 13, 1880, is similar, but it lacks the mirrored back. An armchair design from April 1888 is only slightly different, but it has an optional crest in the shape of a sun with a face on the back (Fig. 3-32b). There is also a "Crystal Throne Chair" with canopy from January 1884. An article on this object was published in a trade journal shortly thereafter. It mentions that the throne chair was made for an Indian client, that it was nine feet six inches tall, and that it featured a dome-shaped canopy of Moorish design. "One of the most interesting features about the work," the writer noted, "is the ingenuity with which the 176 pieces composing the throne have been fitted so as to give it a solidified appearance."[29] Unfortunately, the present location of this piece is unknown.

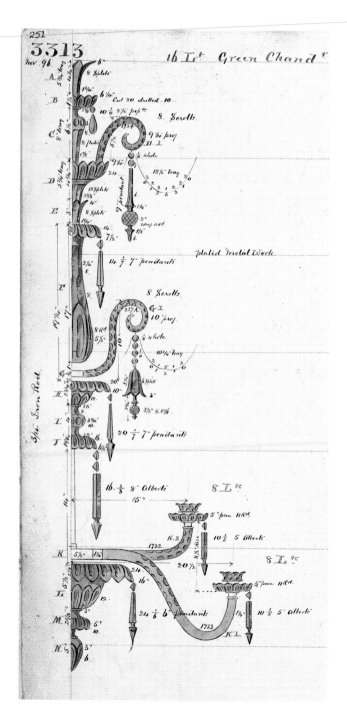

FIGURE 3-28

Design for green chandelier, dated November 1896, from Osler pattern book, v. 1, p. 251. Birmingham Museum and Art Gallery, Birmingham.

FIGURE 3-29

Chandelier with eight arms,
blown, cut, gilded; brass fittings. F. & C. Osler, about
1860–1880. H. 162.8 cm. The
Corning Museum of Glass,
Corning, New York (95.2.13).

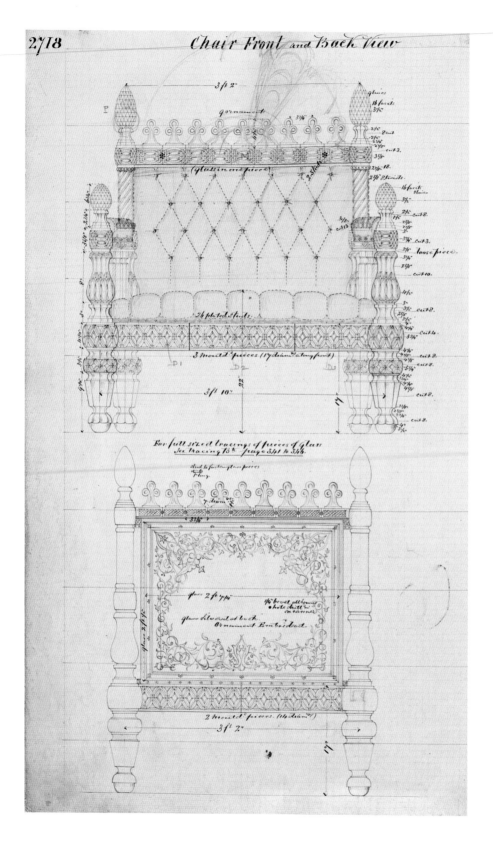

Figure 3-30

Design for glass chair and footstool, 1875–1876, from Osler pattern book, v. 1, p. 145. Birmingham Museum and Art Gallery, Birmingham.

Figure 3-31

Second drawing of glass chair and footstool, 1875–1876, from Osler pattern book, v. 1, p. 146. Birmingham Museum and Art Gallery, Birmingham.

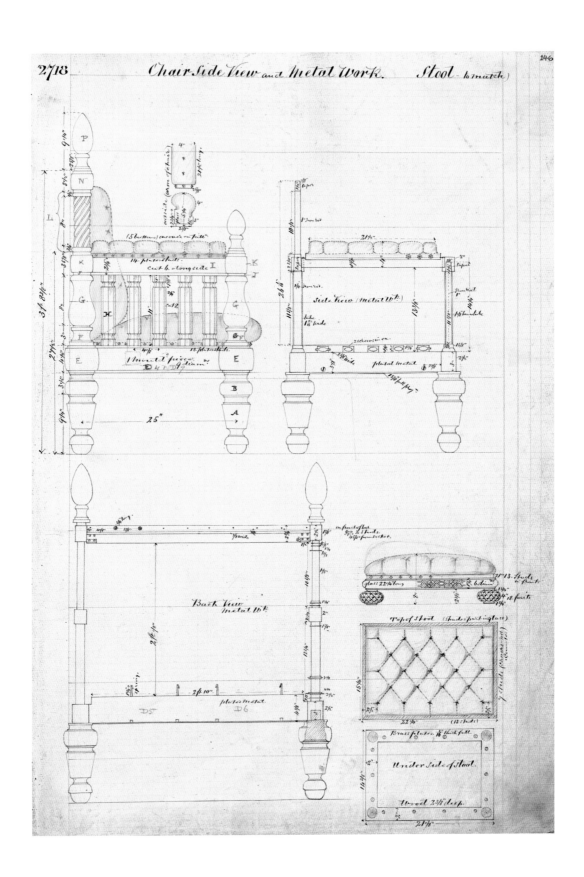

Chair Side View and Metal Work. Stool (to match.)

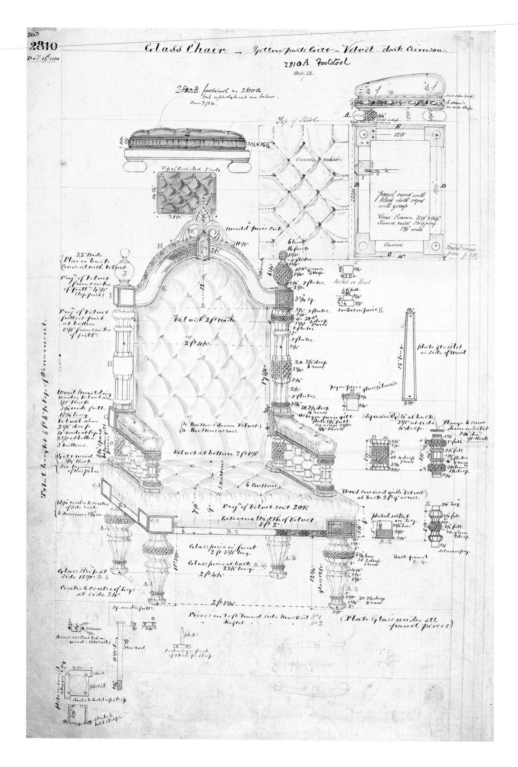

Figure 3-32a

Design for glass chair, dated December 1880, from Osler pattern book, v. 1, p. 163.
Birmingham Museum and Art Gallery, Birmingham.

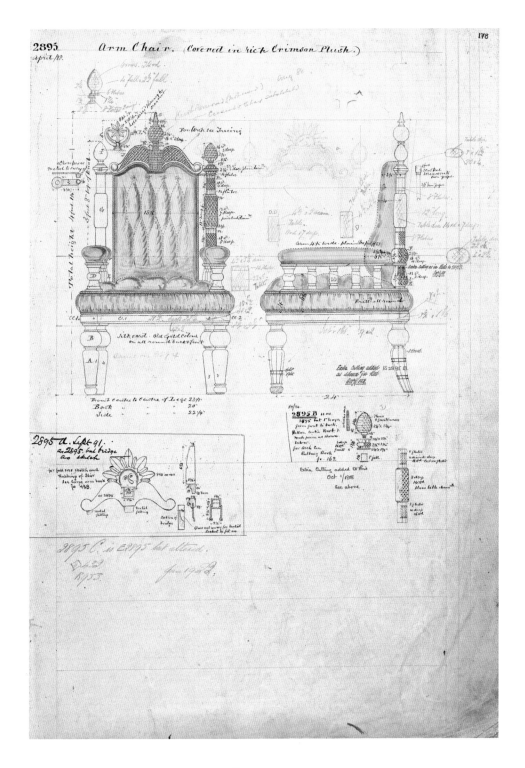

Figure 3-32b

Design for glass chair, dated April 1888, from Osler pattern book, v. 1, p. 178.
Birmingham Museum and Art Gallery, Birmingham.

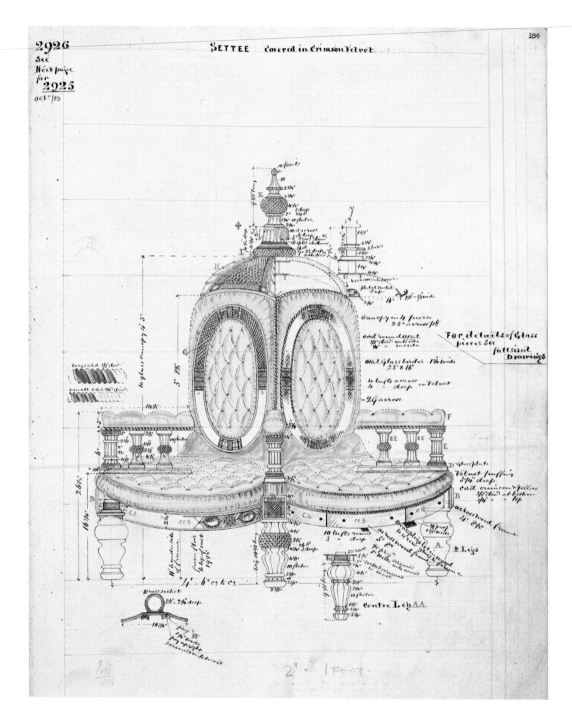

The Osler pattern books contain three designs for a settee, one from October 1883 (Fig. 3-33) and two that are undated but seem to be from after the turn of the 20th century (Figs. 3-34 and 3-35a). Pieces based on both of these later designs can still be seen in India, and the palaces at Udaipur and Patiala have examples of the design shown in Figure 3-35a (Fig. 3-35b). Osler's Indian customers were fond of color, so it is not surprising that all of the chair and settee designs are shown upholstered in

FIGURE 3-33

Design for glass settee, dated October 1883, from Osler pattern book, v. 1, p. 184. Birmingham Museum and Art Gallery, Birmingham.

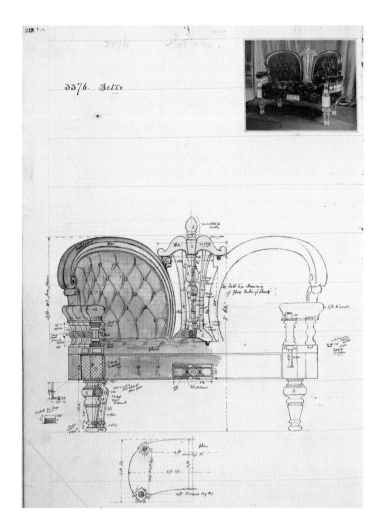

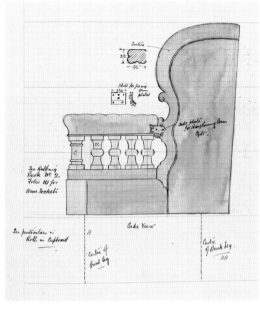

FIGURE 3-34

Design for glass settee, 1900–1910, from Osler pattern book, v. 2, pp. 217 and 218. An original photograph of the settee is attached to the page. Birmingham Museum and Art Gallery, Birmingham.

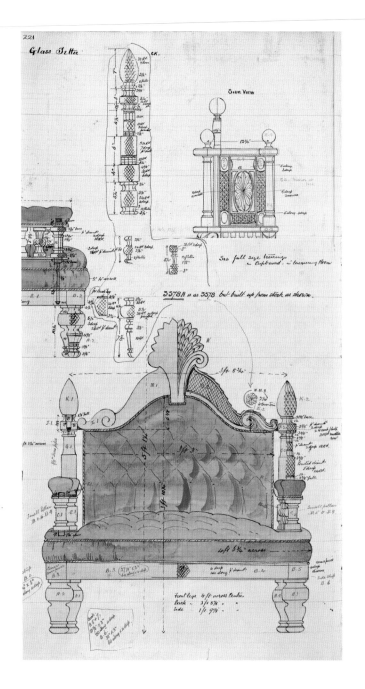

Figure 3-35b

Osler glass settee in the Sheesh Mahal at Motibagh Palace, Patiala, made from design shown in Figure 3-35a.

Figure 3-35a

Design for glass settee, 1900–1910, from Osler pattern book, v. 2, p. 221. Birmingham Museum and Art Gallery, Birmingham.

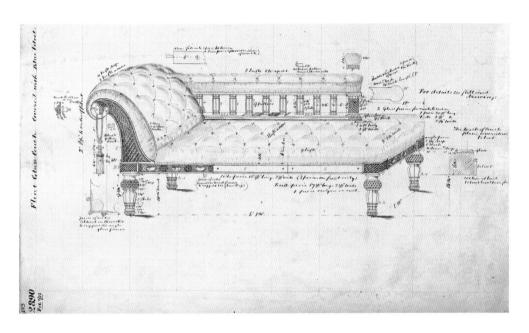

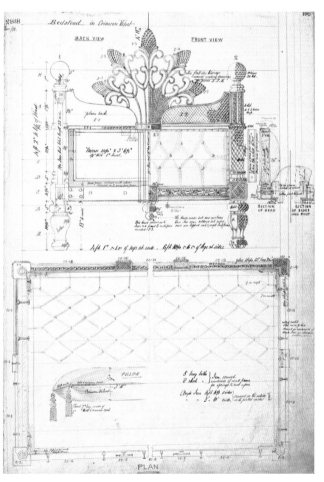

FIGURE 3-36

Design for blue glass couch, dated February 1883, from Osler pattern book, v. 1, p. 173. Birmingham Museum and Art Gallery, Birmingham.

FIGURE 3-37

Design for glass bed, dated November 1882, from Osler pattern book, v. 1, p. 170. Birmingham Museum and Art Gallery, Birmingham.

crimson velvet. Two slightly different designs for couches, dated February 1883, are shown in blue (Fig. 3-36) and in red, and one of them is preserved in the palace at Baroda. There are three designs for beds from 1882 and 1883 (Figs. 3-37 and 3-38a, b) and two for bassinets from 1880 and 1882 (Fig. 3-39).

A newspaper account mentions a "suite of bedroom articles, including a bedstead . . . made for a Spanish nobleman,"[30] so not all of the Osler firm's furniture went to India. Indeed, like other 19th-century European factories, Osler sought orders from among the wealthy in Europe as well as in India.

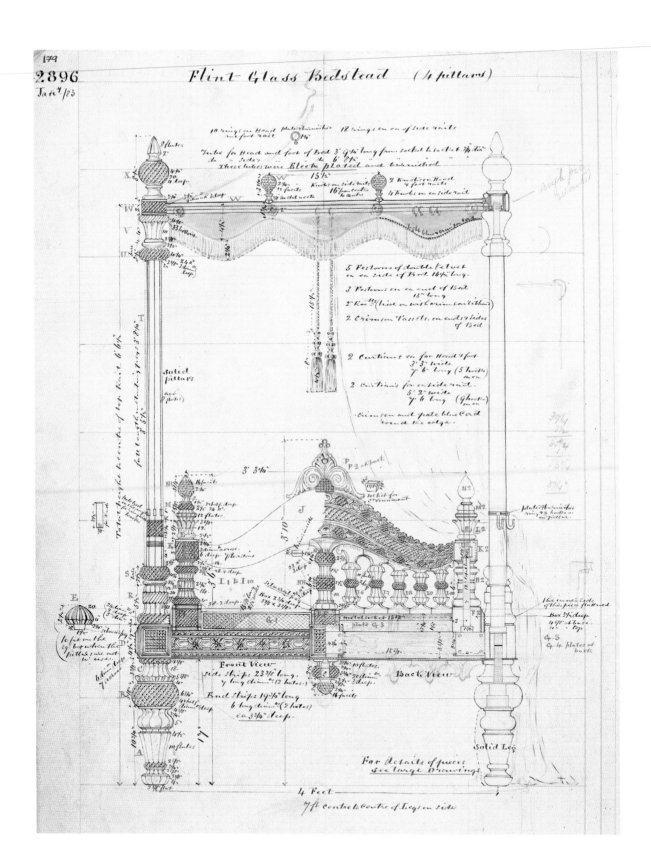

FIGURE 3-38A

Design for glass bed, dated
January 1883, from Osler pattern book, v. 1, p. 179. Birmingham Museum and Art
Gallery, Birmingham.

FIGURE 3-38B

Detail of Osler glass bed in
crystal gallery at City Palace,
Udaipur.

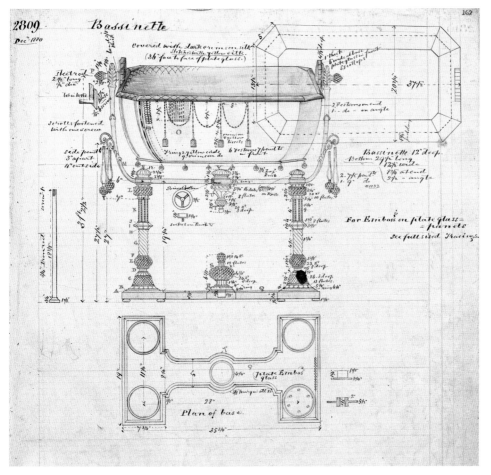

FIGURE 3-39

Design for glass bassinet, dated February 1882, from Osler
pattern book, v. 1, p. 167. Birmingham Museum and Art
Gallery, Birmingham.

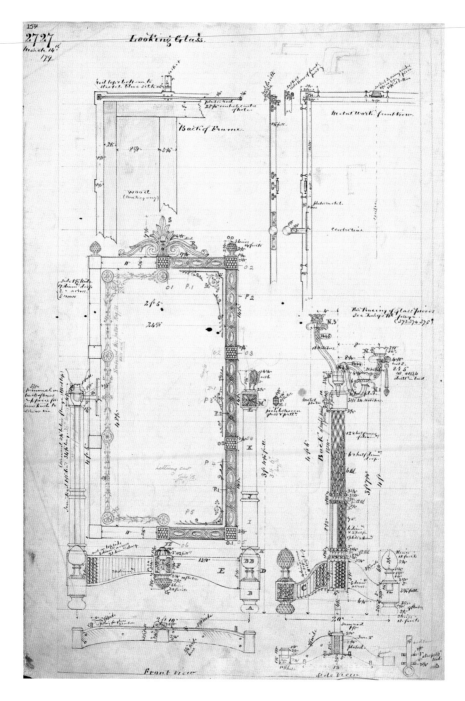

Four designs for looking glasses (Fig. 3-40), ranging in date from 1881 to 1897, can still be seen in various Indian palaces today. The furniture that is not upholstered, such as washstands, large cabinets, and tables in various shapes (Fig. 3-41), is scattered throughout the catalogs, and several of the tables are dated from the first decade of the 20th century. Some of the designs, including library steps covered with glass (Fig. 3-42) and an elaborate overmantel, seem wildly impractical, and they may

Figure 3-40

Design for looking glasses, dated May 1881, from Osler pattern book, v. 1, p. 157. Birmingham Museum and Art Gallery, Birmingham.

Figure 3-41

Design for glass table, 1897–1910, from Osler pattern book, v. 2, unpaged. Birmingham Museum and Art Gallery, Birmingham.

Figure 3-42

Design for glass library steps, dated November 1890, from Osler pattern book, v. 1, p. 219. Birmingham Museum and Art Gallery, Birmingham.

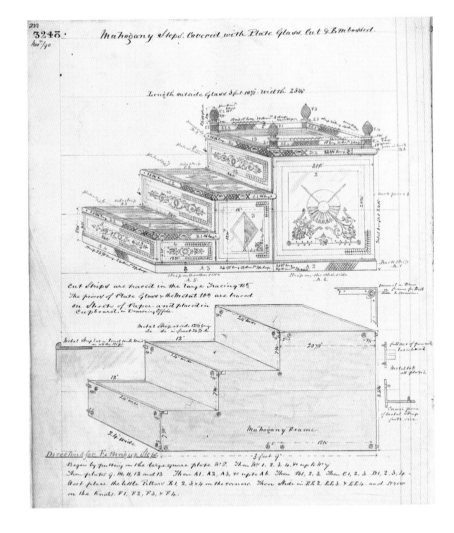

never have been produced. The tables, however, are in several Indian palaces, and some additional examples have turned up in salesrooms during the last 20 years.

The whatnot with three shelves (Fig. 3-43) must have been a popular design because several of them are in the Jai Vilas Palace at Gwalior and at Udaipur, while others have been shown in salesrooms. The design for this object in Osler's pattern book is dated September 1882. The shelves are mirrored, as is a four-tiered corner whatnot that is now in a private collection. A smaller table in The Corning Museum of Glass (Fig. 3-44) is unmarked, but it was almost certainly made by Osler, although it is possible (but unlikely) that it was produced at the factory of Joseph Webb (see

FIGURE 3-45

Fly whisk, cast, cut, polished; electroplated finial, horsehair. F. & C. Osler, about 1875. L. 47.5 cm. The Corning Museum of Glass, Corning, New York (2000.2.3).

FIGURE 3-44

Table, blown, tooled, cut, assembled; silver-plated brass. Probably F. & C. Osler, about 1880–1920. H. 76.2 cm. The Corning Museum of Glass, Corning, New York (2004.2.13).

pages 111–115). Other unmarked tables presumably made by Osler have also appeared on the market. The handle for a fly whisk (Fig. 3-45) is evidently glass produced in Europe for use in India and may also be an Osler product. Elaborately decorated whisks were used in both ceremonial and practical contexts, and are often illustrated in paintings of Indian nobility, being held by the ruler's servant who stands nearby.

Another interesting item made for Osler's Calcutta showroom is a glass carpet (Fig. 3-46), one of a pair that are numbered 3168 in the company's pattern book. Although this design is undated, it must be from the 1880s. These carpets are thought to have been used in the Bhopal Mosque for a number of years.

FIGURE 3-46

Glass carpet made for the Bhopal Mosque, cast, cut, engraved. F. & C. Osler,
about 1885. L. 114 cm. The Corning Museum of Glass, Corning, New York (2000.2.2).

One design that was made several times over two decades is the 18-light candelabrum shown in Figure 3-47. This was originally designed for kerosene in 1881, adapted for candles in 1883, and made for electricity in the 1890s.

On the basis of the design books, it is clear that these imposing pieces remained popular until World War I. Although no new designs are dated after that time, pieces were occasionally reordered. At least two grandfather clocks were made to the same design in 1910 and 1924, and two designs for chandeliers are dated 1923 and 1924.

A decline in sales forced Osler to close its glass factory in 1922. Although the company continued to make lighting devices from glass purchased elsewhere, as it had done in its early years, it no longer had the facilities to make furniture. The firm remained in business until the 1970s, but on a much smaller scale, and most of its designs after 1920 were for metal objects with glass fittings.

All of the Osler pieces illustrated in this chapter are designs that were well suited to the Western-style palaces constructed by Indian rulers in the late 19th and early 20th centuries. However, their emphasis on color and the reflective quality of the glass ensured that they would never enjoy a similar popularity in English houses of that time, for English sensibilities continued to favor colorless glass with a high refractive index and simple designs.

FIGURE 3-47

Candelabrum with 18 candle arms, blown, cut; white marble plinth. F. & C. Osler (design no. 2811), about 1883. H. 295 cm. The Corning Museum of Glass, Corning, New York (96.2.10). The original design, dated June 1881, had six kerosene lamps, but Osler adapted it for candles in October 1883. It was later made for electricity as well.

Jonas Defries & Sons

ONE OF THE LARGEST but least-known 19th-century English glass firms is Jonas Defries & Sons, which was located in the Houndsditch section of London from 1856 until the early 20th century (Fig. 4-1). The company operated under various names for at least a century (an 1880 advertisement says that it was established in 1803),[1] so the lack of information about it is surprising. Its production focused on lighting, much of it for large-scale commercial use in theaters and other public buildings, but no marked wares have been found. Defries did not make much glass furniture, although it did register designs for two pieces. Its chandeliers and candelabra are of interest because the firm actively sought customers in the Near and Far East. A prismatic mirror—one of eight made for the Turkish sultan's palace—was registered by Defries in 1857 and exhibited at the London world's fair of 1862 (see page 26). These mirrors were groundbreaking in their technology, but they were not praised for their design by most critics at that time.

The company sent displays to the expositions of 1855, 1862, and 1867, winning honorable-mention medals at the latter two fairs for the excellence of its large chandeliers and candelabra. These medals were featured in Defries's advertising for the next two decades. The firm maintained both a factory for assembling its pieces and showrooms in London, but it also had a factory in Birmingham, where the glass parts were made.

Defries also exhibited in 1862 what *Cassell's Illustrated Family Paper Exhibitor* referred to as a "Monster Crystal Chandelier," which it hailed as "one of the most striking among the many beautiful objects" in its class. The account continued:

FIGURE 4-1

Design for Jonas Defries & Sons sign, registered November 29, 1880. The National Archives U.K. (TNA(PRO) BT43/63 359014).

This particular chandelier is so colossal in its magnitude, so elaborate in its design and construction, and so unique in its general effect, as to call for a slight description. The 'dome' of the chandelier is surmounted by a Prince of Wales' coronet and plume, all of elaborately cut glass, and supported by eight diamond-cut pillars resting on a vase formed of prisms. Between these pillars is a glass tent comprised of cut diamond spangles. The centre, also, is supported by eight diamond-cut pillars terminating in graceful spires, which also rest on a vase of prisms. . . . The main body of the chandelier consists of richly-cut prisms, or rather truncated pyramids, each 3 feet 6 inches in length—a size, we believe, not before attained in this species of ornamentation. . . . The prismatic vase occupying the centre of the lower columns constitutes a singularly beautiful object in the whole composition. . . . A bouquet of crystal flowers springs from this vase, an effect of no small difficulty to render faithfully, but which has been very cleverly managed.[2]

No illustration matching this description has been found.

The official catalog of the 1862 exhibition describes Defries as making lighting devices of every description "for India and the colonial markets in general."[3] Unfortunately, the firm's advertising does not list other countries, but a Defries catalog dating to the 1860s mentions customers in the Near East. *Cassell's* also illustrated and described a "Grand Glass Candelabrum" that stood 23 feet tall (Fig. 4-2). It characterized this piece as "of magnificent proportions, and . . . really the finest object of the kind in the Exhibition. . . . The whole structure contains so much rich and elaborate cutting, that its appearance when lighted up must be extremely brilliant, while the crowning ornament is so constructed as to intensify the general effect. Messrs. Defries are the manufacturers of the chandelier at the Royal Italian Opera [in Covent Garden, London], and at most of the principal theatres and music halls."[4] Defries also listed the "New Opera" in St. Petersburg as a customer.

Another publication commented, dismissively, on the Defries display as follows: "It is possible that their 'prismatic mirror,' a ton-weight of very ordinary prisms . . . may not appear out of place as an adjunct to the barbaric splendour of an Eastern potentate, and the same may be said of their huge chandelier; but, though the latter has some merit in certain points of manufacture, it would be difficult to find any objects in the Exhibition more obtrusively destitute of artistic merit."[5]

Between 1854 and 1882, the Defries company registered a number of designs for chandeliers and candelabra, and several of them seem to have been made specifically for the Indian market. The two fixtures described above were registered on December 15, 1862 (Figs. 4-3 and 4-4). On December 24 of the following year, Defries registered three designs: the "Alhambra Chandelier for India" (Fig. 4-5), a "Prismatic Chandelier" (Fig. 4-6), and a "Crystal Candelabrum" (Fig. 4-7) that is very similar to the candelabrum displayed at the 1862 exhibition. Defries illustrated all three of these designs in color for the registration. The name "Alhambra"[6] for the first design is probably meant to emphasize its color. Because colored chandeliers were not popular in England, all of these objects were probably intended for the Eastern market. The illustrations of the candelabrum and the prismatic chandelier were accompanied by a picture of the medal won at the fair, where Defries had received an honorable mention for "Chandeliers, lustres, and table glass. For a novel glass screen, a chandelier of colossal dimensions, and specimens of general excellence."[7] Since the pieces that had been shown at the London exposition were made of colorless glass, it is somewhat surprising that the firm chose to register them with colored parts. It is also significant that the 1862 designs are illustrated with gas shades and the 1863 designs are with candle shades. This change also indicates that the later designs were made for the Eastern market.

FIGURE 4-2

"Grand Glass Candelabrum" by Defries, from *Cassell's Illustrated Family Paper Exhibitor* [note 2], p. 204. Juliette K. and Leonard S. Rakow Research Library of The Corning Museum of Glass, Corning, New York.

cut an inch and a half deep. Immediately below this, and supporting the columns just spoken of, comes the main body of the chandelier. From this spring 112 lights. The main body of the chandelier consists of richly-cut prisms, or rather truncated pyramids, each 3 feet 6 inches in length—a size, we believe, not before attained in this species of ornamentation. This arrangement produces a most elegant effect when viewed from below—that of one large prismatic dish, under which two other dishes are formed in a similar way; the whole being terminated with a richly-cut spire. The prismatic vase occupying the centre of the lower columns constitutes a singularly beautiful object in the whole composition, although all the component parts of it are kept in judicious subordination to one another. A bouquet of crystal flowers springs from this vase, an effect of no small difficulty to render faithfully, but which has been

very cleverly managed. We may congratulate the firm on the very satisfactory execution of this fine work, every portion of which has been done upon their own premises. In good taste it is beyond all criticism. We are glad to observe that this and other firms do not perpetuate the error observable in the glass exhibition of 1851, of making chandeliers of coloured glass; for nothing can surpass the iridescent lustre of pure colourless flint glass. This beautiful object, then, displays 168 lights, arranged in two tiers. It is 14 feet in diameter, and 23 feet high, and the glass and metal of which it is composed weigh nearly three tons.

There has been lately placed in the Glass Court the handsome candelabrum here shown. This work is of magnificent proportions, and is really the finest object of the kind in the Exhibition. The base of the entire structure is sexagonal, the angles being occupied by six cut-glass pillars, the central cylinder

GRAND GLASS CANDELABRUM.   MESSRS. DEFRIES AND SONS.   HOUNDSDITCH.

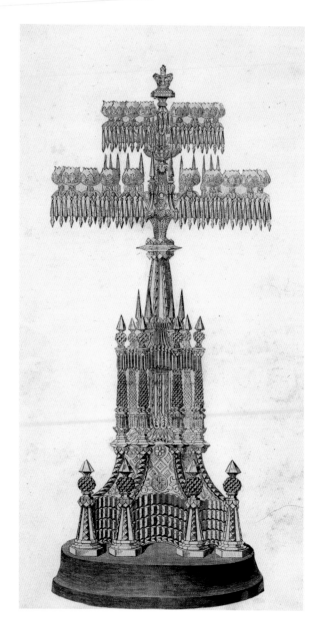

FIGURE 4-5

Design for "Alhambra Chandelier for India" by Defries, registered December 24, 1863. The National Archives U.K. (TNA(PRO) BT43/61 170523).

FIGURE 4-6

Design for "Prismatic Chandelier" by Defries, registered December 24, 1863. The National Archives U.K. (TNA(PRO) BT43/61 170524).

FIGURE 4-7

Design for "Crystal Candelabrum" by Defries, registered December 24, 1863. The National Archives U.K. (TNA(PRO) BT43/61 170525).

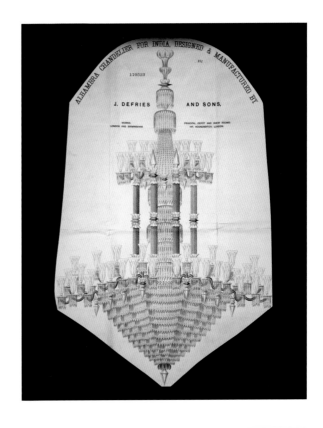

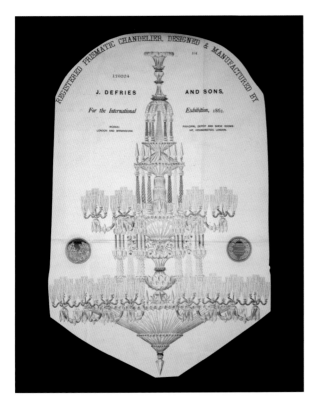

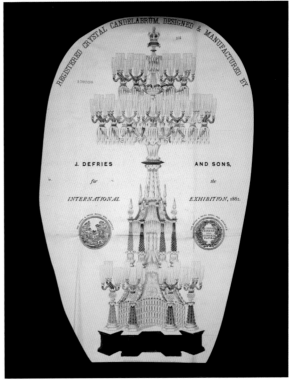

In 1864, Defries registered a design for a glass temple (Fig. 4-8). The illustration submitted with the application shows the object with two men wearing turbans, so the temple was clearly intended for a Turkish or Indian customer. A version of this piece had probably been displayed at the 1862 exhibition as well, since *Cassell's* had commented there on "the gorgeous crystal temple of Defries, which has cost over £3,000 to manufacture."[8] Unfortunately, none of the other publications describing the fair mentioned Defries's temple, so it is impossible to know if it looked like the one in the registered design, or if it was comparable in size. Its buyer is also unknown.

FIGURE 4-8

Design for glass temple by Defries, registered October 24, 1864. The National Archives U.K. (TNA(PRO) BT43/ 61 180385).

FIGURE 4-9

"Crystal Jewelled Candelabrum" by Defries, from
The Illustrated Catalogue of the Universal Exhibition
[note 9], p. 51. Juliette K. and Leonard S. Rakow
Research Library of The Corning Museum of
Glass, Corning, New York.

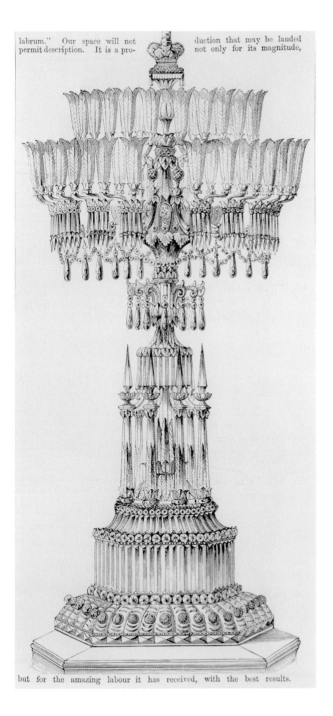

labrum." Our space will not   duction that may be lauded
permit description. It is a pro-   not only for its magnitude,

but for the amazing labour it has received, with the best results.

At the 1867 Exposition Universelle in Paris, the *Art Journal* stated that Defries "have established renown as manufacturers of GLASS CHANDELIERS, especially such as are of large size, and intended for public buildings. Not only in England, but in various parts of Europe, in Asia, and in America, they have supplied 'light' to many huge edifices. . . ."[9] In fact, the firm's 1869–1870 catalog lists more than 20 theaters in London and elsewhere in England that contained chandeliers made by Defries. The Strand Music Hall, for example, was illuminated with gas chandeliers and colored sheets of glass in 1864. One publication commented, "The thorough lighting of all our principal opera houses, theatres, music halls, etc. bear full testimony to the vast resources of Messrs. J. Defries & Sons."[10] Most of the firm's display at the 1867 exhibition focused on tableware, but it did feature a mammoth 18-foot-high "Crystal Jewelled Candelabrum" with 48 candles (Fig. 4-9).

Lighting devices shown by Defries at the 1867 world's fair were the first shown by the company with glass shades for the candles, which probably means that they were intended for export to India. Candle shades on chandeliers were unnecessary in North America and Europe, where drafts from open windows were not common. Most of the company's previous designs had been for gas fixtures made for the European market, while those produced for the Indian market featured candles and had larger shades. Glass companies from several countries exhibited chandeliers for candles at the 1867 world's fair, but only one other firm showed them with shades on the candles. All of the other examples had open candle sockets.

An account of a visit to the large Defries factory in London, published in 1864, reveals how the company originated. "A number of genuine and primitive looms are employed in the manufacture of lamp-cotton [wicks], a business (the nucleus of the present large establishment) which was commenced by the father of the present firm some half century ago. Here, . . . lamp-cottons, both for home consumption and exportation, are made in every variety. . . . Notwithstanding the hundred inventions in lamps, and the various means of artificial light, the 'wicks' for oil-lamps are still in enormous demand, especially in India. . . ."[11] The reporter went on to note "the wonderful array of lamps of every description and at every price, from the more costly and elegantly decorated oil-light for burning under the punkah [ceiling fan] in India to the cheapest form of paraffin-lamp. . . ."[12]

An 1869 Defries catalog, which by this time included the words "By Appointment to HER MOST GRACIOUS MAJESTY, QUEEN VICTORIA, HIS ROYAL HIGHNESS THE PRINCE OF WALES, . . . the Emperor of the French," lists among the firm's customers the palaces of the sultan in Constantinople, the king of Siam, the prince of Surat, the duke of Monpensier in Seville, and the "New Palace of the Nizam of the Deccan, India."[13] At the back of the catalog, a listing of other catalogs for interested customers includes publications devoted to lamps and chandeliers for the Indian market, with the announcement that "gas now being introduced into India, China, and the Colonies, Messrs. J. Defries & Sons . . . call the attention of Merchants and the Trade generally, to their New Book . . . of the most elegant and chaste [simple and refined] designs with the true oriental colors."[14]

Defries clearly set out to invade F. & C. Osler's near monopoly of the Indian market. A letter from Osler's Calcutta office, written in 1868, mentions that "Defries is advertising very largely in India [and] has sent out books of sketches of his goods to every native of any note in India. . . ."[15] Other letters from that office note that Defries's agent visited Bombay in 1871 and describe a proposal from the Defries firm, dated July 28, 1874, when it was competing with Osler for an order from the maharajah of Gwalior, who was building a new palace. One Defries brochure (Fig. 4-10) offers "CHANDELIERS, CANDELABRA, FOUNTAINS & MOSQUES FOR INDIA" and lists "WORKS" in "London, Birmingham & Paris." This particular brochure can be dated because

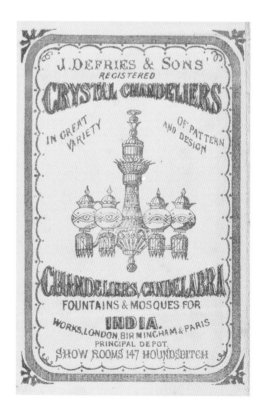

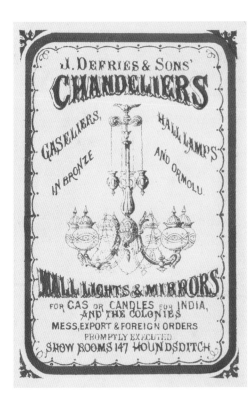

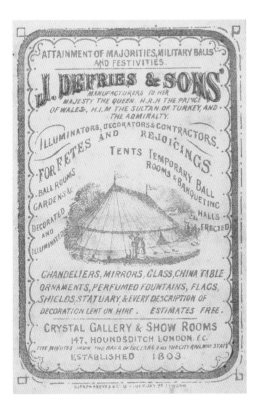

FIGURE 4-10

Panels from a Defries double-sided brochure, about 1871–1880. Shirley Papers, collection of The New Bedford Museum of Glass, New Bedford, Massachusetts.

it illustrates Storer's Patent Perpetual Table Fountain and offers it for "HOME, IN-DIA, & THE COLONIES." The fountain was patented by Joseph Storer in June 1870, and therefore the brochure was probably published in the 1870s. Four of its six pages mention India, so it is obvious that Defries was actively pursuing that market. Unfortunately, no other information about the firm's works in Paris has been found.

Neither of the two designs registered by Defries in the 1870s pertained to glass furniture or lighting, but most of the 19 designs it registered between 1880 and 1883 were for various forms of lighting fixtures. Two designs for glass settees were registered on December 3, 1880 (Figs. 4-11 and 4-12). No pieces of furniture matching these designs have ever been found, but they were probably made for an Indian palace or created on speculation and sold in India. On the same day, another elaborate candelabrum design was registered, and it, too, featured candle shades (Fig. 4-13).

The Osler firm specialized in the production of glass furniture in the 1880s, and it had displayed several pieces at the 1878 world's fair in Paris. The activities of this company may have inspired Defries to compete in the Indian market. That Defries was still doing an active business in India in 1880 is clear from its advertisements in *The Pottery Gazette*, a trade publication, which mention "CRYSTAL GLASS CHANDE-LIERS . . . of every description, to burn gas, kerosine, or candles" and "LAMPS for kerosine . . . Vase Lamps for India."[16] On March 28, 1882, Defries registered two

FIGURE 4-11

Design for glass settee by Defries, registered December 3, 1880. The National Archives U.K. (TNA(PRO) BT43/ 63 359237).

FIGURE 4-12

Design for glass settee by Defries, registered December 3, 1880. The National Archives U.K. (TNA(PRO) BT43/63 359238).

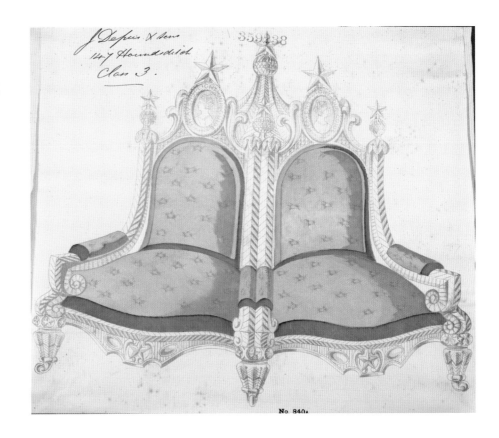

similar designs for Venetian-style chandeliers (Figs. 4-14 and 4-15), which represented a significant departure from anything previously made in England. The following April, Osler registered a very similar design. All three of these objects were very colorful, and they were probably intended for the Eastern market. The Defries firm's last two chandelier designs (Figs. 4-16 and 4-17) were registered on September 26, 1882, and it is impossible to say whether these huge objects were intended for a London theater or an Indian palace.

The 1885 *Post Office London Commercial Directory* describes the Defries company as "manufacturers of crystal, bronzed & ormolu chandeliers, sun & star lights, mediaeval & other gas fittings & gas engineers, electric light fittings & electrolers [sic]; punkah lamp for India[,] petroleum, kerosene & duplex lamps; . . . Hotel & table glass, earthenware, china, ornamental clocks, musical boxes, foreign vases & lustres & fancy ornaments of the most classical & elaborate designs; . . . manufacturers of the patent crystal illuminating devices & variegated lamps in oil & gas. . . ."

This was the largest list of products published for Defries, and it is obvious that the firm was buying table wares of ceramics and glass, as well as other giftware, from other companies for resale. This expansion in the mid-1880s was short-lived, however. Advertisements in *The Pottery Gazette* began to decrease in size, and they disappeared altogether in 1886. That year's *Post Office London Commercial Directory* entry for Defries consisted solely of the firm's name and address, with no listing of prod-

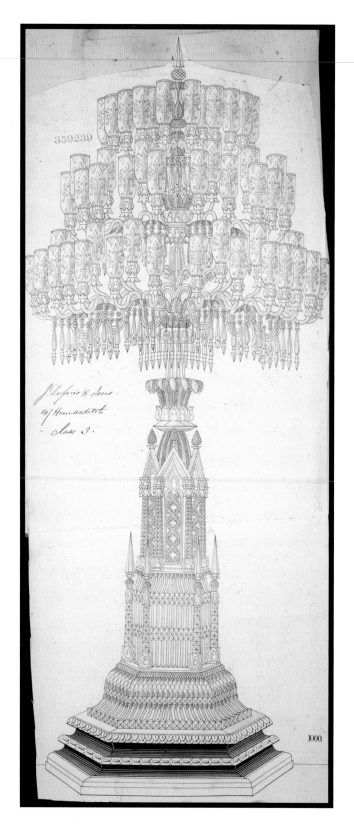

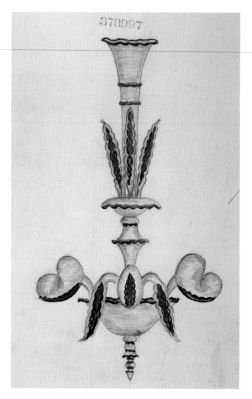

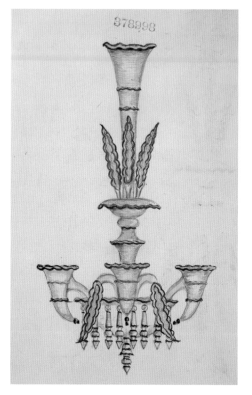

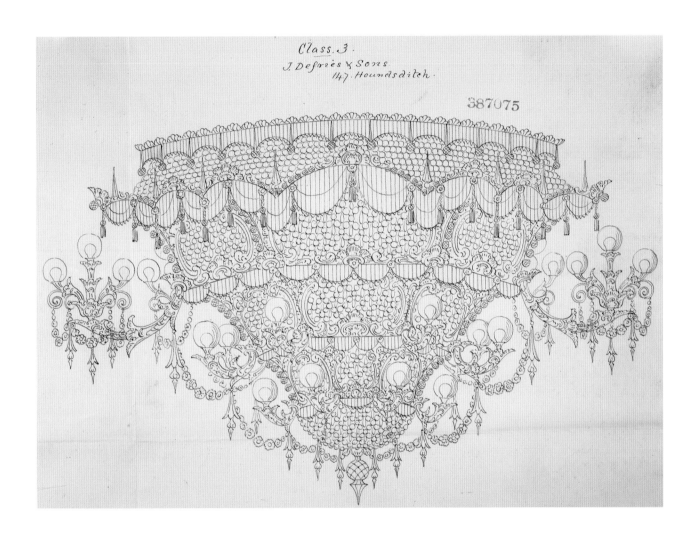

Class. 3.
J. Defries & Sons
147. Houndsditch.

387075

FIGURE 4-13

Design for Defries candelabrum, registered December 3, 1880. The National Archives U.K. (TNA(PRO) BT43/63 359239).

FIGURE 4-14

Design for Venetian-style chandelier of colored glass by Defries, registered March 28, 1882. The National Archives U.K. (TNA(PRO) BT43/63 378997).

FIGURE 4-15

Design for Venetian-style chandelier of colored glass by Defries, registered March 28, 1882. The National Archives U.K. (TNA(PRO) BT43/63 378998).

FIGURE 4-16

Design for chandelier by Defries, registered September 26, 1882. The National Archives U.K. (TNA(PRO) BT43/63 387075).

387077

Class. 3.
J. Defries & Sons.
147 Houndsditch.

ucts. The company may simply have expanded too fast for its market and then been forced to cut back. In 1886, the Defries Safety Lamp and Oil Company Ltd. was started as a new firm, and it produced only the patented safety lamp. The parent company emphasized street and railway lamps in its later, smaller advertisements, and contacts with India were not mentioned. After the turn of the 20th century, Defries began to specialize in lighting for special events as well. Shortly after 1906, the company apparently closed.

The Osler and Baccarat firms had survived Defries's efforts to claim a portion of the Near Eastern market, and they continued to supply India with lighting and furniture when Defries withdrew from competition with them after 1884. Osler remained the principal English supplier for the Indian market.

FIGURE 4-17

Design for gas chandelier by Defries, registered September 26, 1882. The National Archives U.K. (TNA(PRO) BT43/63 387077).

Coalbourne Hill Glass Works

THE THIRD ENGLISH COMPANY that made furniture for the Indian market was located in the Stourbridge area. This factory had been built early in the 19th century, and it was purchased by Joseph Webb in 1850. He was a cousin of Thomas Webb, owner of the famous glass firm of Thomas Webb & Sons, and he had worked there for a time before joining with another cousin to start his own company. At Coalbourne Hill, Joseph Webb made both colorless and colored glass tableware, and he registered a number of designs for pressed glass in the 1850s. Following his death in 1869, his factory was operated by his executors: his widow, Jane Webb, and her brother, Joseph Hammond. During that time, the firm produced mostly pressed glass tableware. When Hammond left the company at the end of 1880, Mrs. Webb and her son, Henry Fitzroy Webb, assumed control of the factory.[1]

In the early 1880s, the Coalbourne Hill works also made cut glass furniture for the Eastern market. Several years ago, photographs of an armchair and a chaise longue were discovered in the files of another Stourbridge glasshouse, Stuart & Sons, along with a costing sheet dated August 30, 1880, and a note stating that the chair was delivered on January 7, 1881. Accompanying this material were some sketches of whatnots.[2] Although there is nothing in these documents that identifies them as belonging to the Webb company, the photographs match pieces shown in a full-page advertisement from the *Golden Guide to London* of 1884 (Fig. 5-1). An 1883 article in an American trade journal reports that "this firm . . . also makes a specialty of glass furniture. These are beautifully upholstered suites, and what is usually woodwork is substituted by elaborately cut crystal."[3] Fortunately, several examples that match the photographs and advertisement are in the Jai Vilas Palace in Gwalior: chairs (Fig. 5-2), two chaise longues (Fig. 5-3), and a *borne* (a French circular sofa); (Fig. 5-4).[4] The footstool in Figure 5-2 is not shown in the *Golden Guide* advertisement, but it clearly matches the other Webb furniture at Gwalior. In these pieces, glass parts were added to what is primarily wooden furniture, and aside from the legs, they do not support the objects structurally, but instead serve a purely decorative function.

A large order for this furniture is described in an article that was written the following year:

> On a visit to Stourbridge during the past month, we had the pleasure of seeing, in an advanced state of completion, a magnificent glass cheffonier [*sic*]

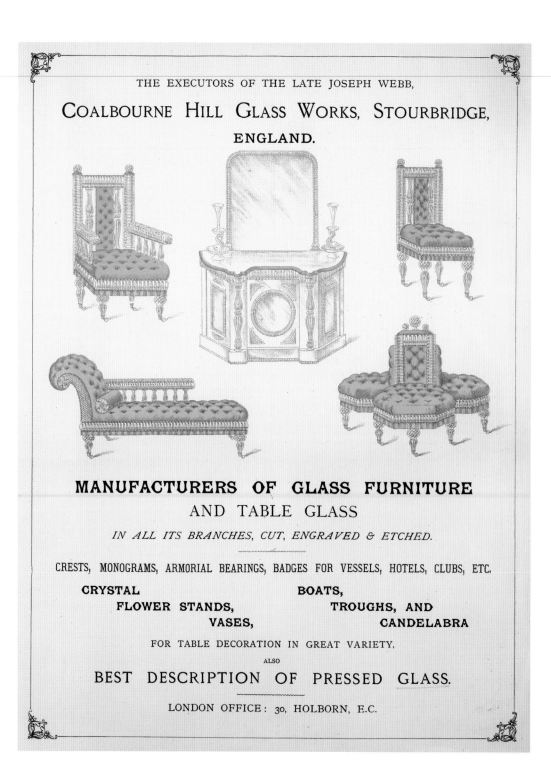

FIGURE 5-1

Full-page advertisement for glass furniture. From *Golden Guide to London*, 1884. Juliette K. and Leonard S. Rakow Research Library of The Corning Museum of Glass, Corning, New York.

FIGURE 5-2

Glass armchairs and footstool. Coalbourne Hill Glass Works, about 1880–1886. Jai Vilas Palace, Gwalior.

FIGURE 5-3

Glass chaise longue. Coalbourne Hill Glass Works, about 1880–1886. Jai Vilas Palace, Gwalior.

FIGURE 5-4

Suite of glass furniture including a *borne* (circular sofa). Coalbourne Hill Glass Works, about 1880–1886. The étagères, chair, and mirror shown on the right were made by F. & C. Osler about 1880–1900. Jai Vilas Palace, Gwalior.

made by the Executors of the late Joseph Webb, of Coalbourn [*sic*] Hill, Glass Works. But to adequately describe the beautiful suite of cut crystal glass furniture, upholstered in crimson satin, that we also saw, would be extremely difficult. The design is of a medieval kind, and what, under ordinary circumstances, would be a display of artistically carved woodwork is here represented in chastefully-cut crystal glass. The harmony in the colours employed for decoration, leaves nothing to be desired, and the whole reflects the highest credit on the firm producing it, while at the same time, it is another proof of the rapid strides that are being made in the development of the glass-making industry. We understand that the suite referred to is intended for an Oriental court.[5]

Later that year, another article in the same publication made it clear that the production of cut glass furniture at the firm was an ongoing enterprise:

We have recently had the pleasure of inspecting a magnificent billiard table, the entire frame work of which is made of richly cut crystal glass. It has been manufactured by the executors of the late Joseph Webb, of Stourbridge, for a wealthy East India merchant. The work is very finely executed, and the effect when lit up by a brilliant light, is truly beautiful. This enterprising firm has been very successful lately in obtaining orders from India for crystal glass furniture, and they have now, we understand, another billiard table in hand, in addition to a suite of chairs, settees, sofas, &c. We are pleased to see Stourbridge coming to the front with this class of work, which we believe has hitherto had its home in Birmingham, and wi[s]h the Executors of the late Joseph Webb every success in the new branch of trade they have taken up. Drawings of the billiard table and other furniture may be seen at their London showrooms, 30, Holborn, E.C.[6]

Unfortunately, the drawings mentioned in the article have not survived. Because the company closed only two years later, it is unlikely that very much glass furniture was made, and none of the billiard tables has been located. If such furniture was in production for six years, as seems to be suggested by the trade paper accounts, more of it may turn up in other locations in India. At least one of the chaise longues and a side chair were at auction at Sotheby's in London on June 12, 2002. Therefore, the Jai Vilas Palace could not have been the only customer.

What prompted Mrs. Webb and her son to enter this branch of the business remains a mystery, but she may have been attracted by Osler's success, or perhaps her company's pressed glassware was selling well in India. There is no evidence that the Webb firm ever had a showroom in India. Moreover, its principal product, pressed glass tableware, was inexpensive and designed for a completely different market. For these reasons, it would be interesting to know how the company's glass furniture was sold. It may be that the attempt to make and market this furniture led to the closing of the firm in 1886.

Baccarat

THE COMPAGNIE des Verreries et Cristalleries de Baccarat, the most famous name in French glass, was founded in 1764 by Monseigneur de Montmorency-Laval, the bishop of Metz, as a way to utilize the wood on the heavily forested land of his estate. In its early years, the factory operated under the name Verreries de Sainte-Anne (after the patron saint of the glassworks' chapel). It was built in the small town of Baccarat, near Lunéville in Lorraine, and its location along the river Meurthe provided ready transportation for raw materials and finished wares.

Economic changes stemming from the French Revolution and the subsequent Napoleonic Wars made production and sales difficult, and the factory changed hands several times before it was acquired by Aimé-Gabriel d'Artigues, owner of a glass factory in the Belgian town of Vonêche. At the king's request, D'Artigues began to make lead glass at Baccarat, the type of glass he had been producing in Belgium. Although he supplied parts to Marie-Jeanne-Rosalie Désarnoud-Charpentier, manager of L'Escalier de Cristal (see page 13), he did not manufacture his own glass furniture or other large pieces. When his health declined, he sold his factory in 1823.

Baccarat was awarded gold medals for tableware and chandeliers it exhibited at several national expositions in Paris between the 1820s and the 1840s. In 1832, Baccarat and a rival glasshouse, the Compagnie des Cristalleries de St. Louis in Moselle, joined with Parisian wholesalers to create Launay, Hautin & Cie. This firm operated showrooms in Paris and was the exclusive outlet for the products of both glasshouses until 1857, when it was dissolved. From that time, Baccarat's own warehouse and workshops were located at Launay's former address. Maintaining impressive Parisian showrooms was vital to French glass manufacturers, especially those that wanted to expand their markets outside the country. In the 1830s, when colored glass and pressed glass were added to Baccarat's product line, the company actively sought new customers in other parts of Europe and in North and South America. By then, the factory employed about 700 workers.

At the 1855 world's fair in Paris, Baccarat displayed a pair of candelabra that stood more than 17½ feet tall. Each was equipped with 90 candles. There was also a 16-foot chandelier. One publication commented: "Nearly opposite MM. Halphen's . . . is a Nave stall glistening with splendid specimens of French glass manufactures. The most prominent contributions to this stall are the two great green and white candelabra sent by the Compagnie des Cristalleries de Baccarat. These immense piles of solid glass are continually compared with the great candelabrum by Osler. . . . The balustrade of this stall is of malachite crystal."[1] This is the first recorded use of color in the making of these mammoth candelabra. The English firms of F. & C. Osler and Jonas Defries & Sons had followed suit by the 1860s.

French influence in the Near East was strong in the 1860s and 1870s. Eugénie, empress of France from 1853 to 1871, visited Cairo and Constantinople. Both the sultan of Turkey and the khedive (Turkish viceroy) in Egypt acquired large chandeliers and candelabra from Baccarat. The shah of Persia, Nāṣer od-Dīn, presented the company with a large order for lighting devices in 1873. Baccarat worked hard to expand its Near Eastern market, and it welcomed wealthy foreign visitors to its Paris showrooms.[2]

The first piece of furniture made by Baccarat appears to have been a small table, the design of which can still be found in the company's files (Fig. 6-1). The drawing is dated 1861, and it indicates that the table was two feet four inches tall and two feet five inches in diameter. This was about the same size as the table displayed by the English glass decorating company of W. P. and G. Phillips at the London exposition of 1862 (see Figure 1-10, page 21). Of these two designs, the one by Baccarat is much more conventional. It has a cut pedestal and top, with a brass base below the foot. No examples of this table have been found.

Baccarat designs for large standing oil lamps dating from the same period also survive in the company's archives. These were very colorful objects, and they may well have been made for the Eastern market. Several of Istanbul's royal palaces have candelabra that were probably manufactured by Baccarat (Fig. 6-2). They consist of cut glass pieces supported on a metal stem, and they resemble lighting devices made by Osler. These objects were likely made in the 1860s or early 1870s.

When Paris hosted its second world's fair, in 1867, the centerpiece of Baccarat's exhibit was a fountain standing 24 feet tall, with a basin 10 feet in diameter (Fig. 6-3). It did not receive the kind of attention that was accorded Osler's Crystal Fountain in 1851, probably because it was neither the first nor the largest such fountain. Baccarat's 1867 display also included a pair of classical vases that were five feet in height. Although these vases were in the company's Paris showrooms for a number of years, they have since disappeared, and there is no record of the purchaser.

Baccarat's display at the third Parisian world's fair, held in 1878, featured the Temple of Mercury (Fig. 6-4), which was 16 feet high and 17 feet in diameter. The temple enclosed a bronze statue of the god Mercury. It remained in the company's

FIGURE 6-1

Design for four-part glass table decorated with cutting, dated 1861. H. 71.1 cm. Baccarat archives, Baccarat.

FIGURE 6-2

Candelabrum probably made by Baccarat, 1860–1875. Dolmabahçe Palace, Istanbul.

European Glass Furnishings for Eastern Palaces

possession until 1892, when it was sold. It is now on the grounds of a private home in northern Spain, along with two five-foot glass vases that are very similar to those presented at the 1867 exposition. Illustrations of Baccarat's 1878 exhibit show an array of very large chandeliers and candelabra, as well as a great deal of tableware. Its most unusual piece, however, was a liqueur cabinet in which the container for the decanters was mounted in an elephant's howdah (Fig. 6-5).[3] It was inspired by the Elephant of the Bastille, a fountain symbolizing French strength that was commissioned by Napoleon I in 1808 but never built. Baccarat produced only a few of these cabinets, but at least one of them was sold in India in the 1880s. It was bought by the maharajah of Baroda, who later purchased glass furniture from Osler. The cabinet displayed at the world's fair is now located in the lobby of the Hôtel Crillon in Paris.

EUROPEAN GLASS FURNISHINGS FOR EASTERN PALACES

The 24-light candelabrum shown in Figure 6-6 features a four-part foot, which Baccarat employed extensively in the 1880s for candelabra. This foot is similar to the tripod foot that was employed on gueridons (small, round tables). The candelabrum was originally designed for display at the world's fair of 1867 or 1878, and it was in production until World War I (the later models were made for electricity). Examples of this lighting device can be found in private collections and in the company's museum in Baccarat. The foot is quite distinctive. The cut patterns on the stem pieces vary, but the shapes are always the same. These were probably standard products rather than specially ordered items. The gueridon was also cut in different patterns (Fig. 6-7), and its design is dated 1883. Photographs in the company's archives show the same base with a cut punch bowl instead of the tabletop. Baccarat created several reproductions of the gueridon in 1993.

FIGURE 6-7

Gueridon (small, round table), pressed, cut, assembled;
central metal shaft. Baccarat,
designed in 1883. Private collection.

The earliest design for glass seating in the Baccarat archives is a drawing for a glass side chair dated 1883 (Fig. 6-8a). It resembles Osler-made chairs, with cut glass pieces assembled on a metal frame, but the stretchers across the legs are a feature that does not appear in the English firm's designs. According to company records, at least one of these chairs was made for María Cristina, queen regent of Spain. Two copies of this chair were in a private collection in Paris in the 1970s, and they are shown in a photograph in the Baccarat archives. In 1993, Baccarat reissued a few copies of this chair (Fig. 6-8b), along with a footstool (Fig. 6-9), copied from the company's original designs. A couch and armchair designed in 1885 match the design of the 1883 chair. Unfortunately, the purchaser of these pieces is unknown, but they may have been sold in the Eastern market. At any rate, Baccarat opened a showroom in Bombay in the 1880s.

The Baccarat files also contain a pen and ink design for a large armchair (Fig. 6-10), the result of a commission for a glass throne. Again, the name of the buyer is not recorded, but this object was certainly made for sale in India.

Company records indicate that Baccarat transported its glass furniture by elephant to customers in India. By 1872, the firm was selling more glass abroad than at home, and much of its market was located in Asia.

The largest pieces of Baccarat furniture were created in 1889. The company's Paris showroom ordered two rectangular tables. Detailed drawings of these pieces (design no. 4923) survive in the firm's archives, but they do not indicate the material from which the top was made. In 1905, one of these two tables, or a third one with a marble

FIGURE 6-8A

Design for glass side chair by Baccarat, dated 1883. The chair was assembled from pressed and cut pieces. Baccarat archives, Baccarat.

FIGURE 6-8B

Side chair made from Baccarat's 1883 design in 1993, incorporating 38 pieces of pressed and cut glass. H. 90 cm, W. 60 cm. Gallery-Museum Baccarat, Paris.

FIGURE 6-9

Footstool made from Baccarat's 1883 design in 1993, molded, cut. H. 48 cm, L. 48 cm. This object was assembled from 26 pieces. Gallery-Museum Baccarat, Paris.

FIGURE 6-10

Baccarat's 1886 design for a glass throne that is thought to have been made for an Indian customer. Baccarat archives, Baccarat.

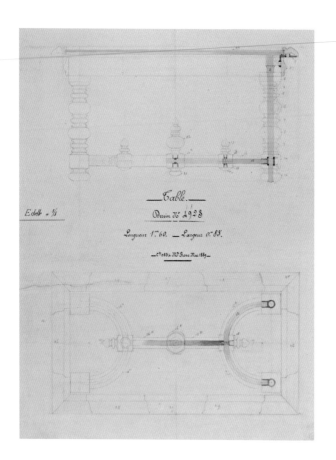

Table.

Dessin N° 4923

Longueur 1.ᵐ60. — Largeur 0.ᵐ85.

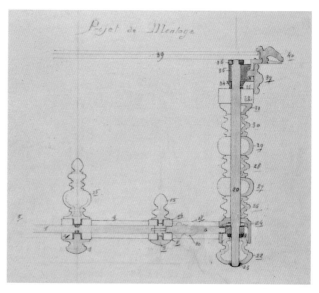

Table d= N°: 4923

FIGURE 6-11

Design for rectangular glass
table by Baccarat, dated 1889.
Baccarat archives, Baccarat.

FIGURE 6-12

Cut glass sculpture in the form of a boat mounted on glass table with a marble top, pressed, cut; assembled on metal frame. Boat designed by Charles Vital Cornu and created by Baccarat in 1900; table designed (with glass top) by Baccarat in 1889. OH. 167 cm. The Corning Museum of Glass, Corning, New York (79.3.155). The table may be one of two that were made in 1889 with a glass top, in which case the top was redone about 1905, or it may be a third table that was made with a marble top between 1900 and 1905 to hold the sculpture.

top, was still in the showroom. It can be seen in a photograph taken there during a visit from Nāṣer od-Dīn, the shah of Persia. By 1927, two Baccarat tables were in the collection of the baroness E. d'Erlanger. One of these pieces, illustrated in an article about her apartment, had a glass top.[4]

At the 1900 world's fair in Paris, the Parisian department store Le Grand Dépôt displayed a sculpture in the form of a boat. It was designed by Charles Vital Cornu (1851–1927) and created in glass and bronze by Baccarat. Following the exposition, this sculpture remained in Baccarat's shop until it was purchased in 1930 by Sri Ganga Singhji Bahadur, the maharajah of Bikaner. It is housed today in the Lallgarh Palace in Bikaner. The maharajah was one of Baccarat's regular customers, and the palace contains several examples of pieces made by the company. Another boat produced by the factory remained there for some years, and it is not known when it was sold. It was part of a lot with a rectangular glass table (Fig. 6-11) that was offered for sale at a Parisian auction in 1979, and both of these objects are now in the collection of The Corning Museum of Glass. The company's records do not state when these pieces were united (Fig. 6-12), but it seems likely that they were together in the Baccarat showroom after 1900, and they were probably purchased at the same time.

Baccarat was an extensive producer of glass chandeliers and candelabra, and many of these objects were sold in Turkey and India. However, it did not follow the example of the Osler and Defries firms in making many colored examples of these pieces. Another customer for Baccarat's large lighting devices was Russia's Czar Nicholas II. He ordered his first candelabrum in 1896, selecting a design from 1878. Although the design was for 79 candles, the czar wanted to have it made for electricity. The Russian royal family continued to order table services and large lighting devices from Baccarat. In fact, it placed so many orders that the firm devoted an entire workshop to filling them. Following the collapse of the czarist government during the Russian Revolution in 1917, Baccarat was left with a pair of candelabra that had been ordered by the royal family. These objects, made between 1905 and 1908, are still in the Baccarat showrooms today. Several pieces based on this design are thought to have been ordered for the company's Indian showroom as well.

Baccarat never manufactured glass furniture on a scale comparable to that attained by the Osler firm. However, while it commanded a much smaller share of the Indian market, that seems to have been the place where most of its furniture and large lighting devices were sold. After World War I, the demand for such sizable pieces declined. Of all the companies that manufactured glass furniture, Baccarat is the only one that is still in business, and its tableware and chandeliers are sold worldwide.

Elias Palme

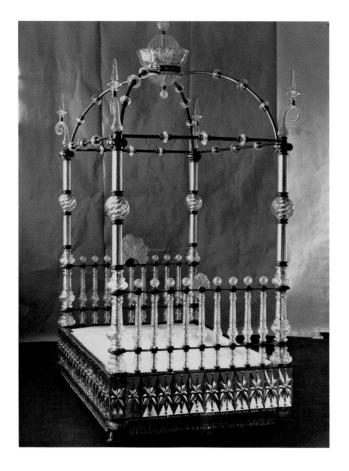

THE FIRM OF ELIAS PALME, one of several companies started by members of the Palme (or Pallme) family, was founded in Kamenický Šenov, Bohemia, in 1849. Most of the Palmes were glass cutters and engravers, and chandeliers were their principal products. Catalogs show table- and floor-size bronze and glass lighting devices, as well as wall-mounted sconces. Like most of the other 19th-century Bohemian glass companies, Elias Palme made much of its glass for export to the rest of Europe, the United States, and the Near East.

In 1894, the firm received an order for a large set of cut glass furniture for one of the palaces of the nizam, the ruler of Hyderabad in southern India, who was then the richest man in the world. The order is documented by an account of Harry Palme, the son of the factory's owner.[1] It is unknown why this order was placed with the Palme company and not with a much larger and better-known firm such as Osler or Baccarat. It is possible, however, that the customer was familiar with Palme-made chandeliers. At that time, Palme had no experience in the design and manufacture of cut glass furniture, but the firm's directors[2] concluded that the prestige attached to such an order would make it worth their while to try to fill it.

Having produced a table and a chair in a month-long trial run, they were prepared to sign a contract that called for several rooms full of furniture, including large and small tables, desks, sofas, armchairs, stools, dressing tables, double beds with canopies and night stands, tables with fish glasses, room fountains, one- and two-seat swings, narghile (hookah) sets, low smoker tables, and balustrades to separate rooms. The only designs offered by the nizam were some pictures of wooden furniture that he wished to have copied in glass. Some of the pieces were to be equipped with music boxes, and several were to be set with jewels supplied by the customer.

This order occupied most of the factory's employees for almost a year. Some of the items had to be ordered elsewhere: music boxes from Switzerland, silk for the chair covers from Liberec, embroideries for other decoration from a school in Sarajevo, and glass fountains from another company in Bohemia. In addition, the jewels obtained from India required special security arrangements that the glass factory was not designed to provide on its own. Nevertheless, the company was able to surmount these difficulties and to complete the order. Its success is attested by photographs that show some of the pieces (Figs. 7-1–7-6). Because the nizam died the following year, no additional pieces were ordered, but he is said to have wanted a carriage made of glass.

FIGURE 7-2

Settee, table, and two chairs made for the nizam's palace, Hyderabad. Elias Palme, about 1895. Národní Technické Muzeum, Prague.

FIGURE 7-4

Dressing table made for the nizam's palace, Hyderabad. Elias Palme, about 1895. Národní Technické Muzeum, Prague.

FIGURE 7-3

Swing made for the nizam's palace, Hyderabad. Elias Palme, about 1895. Národní Technické Muzeum, Prague.

FIGURE 7-5

Etagère made for the nizam's palace, Hyderabad. Elias Palme, about 1895. Národní Technické Muzeum, Prague.

FIGURE 7-6

Armchair made for the nizam's palace, Hyderabad. Elias Palme, about 1895. Národní Technické Muzeum, Prague.

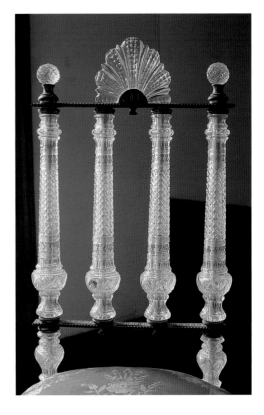

FIGURE 7-7

Chair, with detail showing
glass uprights and finials.
Elias Palme, about 1895–
1900. Dolmabahçe Palace,
Istanbul, Turkey.

One side chair matching those shown in the photographs is now housed in the
Glass Museum in Kamenický Šenov. It is elaborately upholstered in beads.[3] A second
example is in the collection of the Dolmabahçe Palace in Istanbul (Fig. 7-7). This may
mean that the Hyderabad order has been dispersed, but it may also indicate that
Palme filled other orders for this type of furniture. Like Coalbourne Hill, this was a
relatively small company, and it took considerable pride in the successful completion
of the staggering Hyderabad order. However, it did not make furniture after 1900.

Epilogue

The manufacture of large cut glass fountains, furniture, and lighting devices was a late 19th-century phenomenon. These objects were made primarily for sale to Turkey, India, and other eastern countries where the penchant for glitter differed sharply from the more conservative tastes of wealthy consumers in England and France. Such pieces, created by only a few companies in relatively small numbers, were much admired, especially in the East.

Westerners were less enthusiastic. Sir Edwin Lutyens (1869–1944), the English architect, visited Udaipur and remarked that "their taste is for all that glitters. The cut glass furniture, chairs, beds, tables and Huge looking glasses make one squirm. A four poster bed . . . [was] made of white cut glass of the worst sort."[1]

During her trip around the world in 1922, the American writer Dorothy Dix (1870–1951) visited several rulers in India. She was in Udaipur for several days as the guest of the maharana,[2] and she was most impressed by the City Palace. She wrote: "The rooms in the palace are of noble proportions, with an enchanting view across the green lake, but they were furnished entirely in cut glass, and our amazed vision never got beyond that. A reception-room had chairs of cut glass with purple velvet cushions and a table of cut glass. A dining-room had a huge table with cut glass legs and a bevelled glass mirror. . . . A bedroom had a cut glass bed, a four-poster with blue velvet mattress and pink velvet pillows, and in every room there were dozens of hideous cut glass chandeliers in violent colours. Some cut glass salesman must have made a killing at Udaipur."[3]

Turkey became a republic in 1922, and although its first president lived in the Dolmabahçe Palace, he no longer added to its elaborate furnishings. Indian royalty continued to build and occupy magnificent palaces, to visit Europe, and to spend money on motorcars and other European imports, but styles had changed. The production of glass tables continued, but after 1920, they were made in the much simpler Art Deco style. Neither Osler nor Baccarat recorded any furniture orders after 1924, although several glass-topped tables produced in the new style by the French glassmaker René Lalique (1860–1945) can still be found in Indian palaces.

Despite their fragility, these stunning pieces of glass furniture were well maintained by their owners. This careful attention has ensured their survival, permitting modern-day viewers to appreciate them anew. While their elaborate decoration makes them impractical for modern homes, we can admire their imaginative union of technology and design, which is characteristic of the Victorian era. In fact, the current popularity of this furniture with collectors has led to the making of reproductions in India that are now being sold in England and the United States—a geographical reversal of their original manufacture.

Endnotes

FOREWORD

PAGES 6–7

1. Great Exhibition of the Works of Industry of All Nations (1851), *The Crystal Palace Exhibition, Illustrated Catalogue, London, 1851: An Unabridged Republication of The Art-Journal*, New York: Dover Publications Inc., 1970, p. 255.

2. London International Exhibition (1862), *The Record of the International Exhibition, 1862*, gen. ed. Robert Mallet, Glasgow: W. MacKenzie, [1862], p. 409.

3. *The Pottery and Glass Trades' Journal*, v. 1, no. 8, August 1878, p. 116.

CHAPTER 1

Glass Furniture
in the 19th Century

PAGES 8–21

1. Robert J. Charleston, *Masterpieces of Glass: A World History from The Corning Museum of Glass*, New York: Harry N. Abrams Inc., 1980, p. 179. The furniture was described in a letter written from Padua: "I was showed (of their own invention) a set of furniture, in a taste entirely new; it consists of eight large armed-chairs, the same number of sconces, a table, and prodigious looking-glass, all of glass. It is impossible to imagine their beauty; they deserve being placed in a prince's dressing-room, or grand cabinet; the price demanded is £400."

2. *Eglomisé* is a decorative technique in which gold or silver leaf is applied to the back side of a piece of glass, engraved, and protected by varnish, metal foil, or another piece of glass. The name is derived from the French mirror and picture framer Jean-Baptiste Glomy (d. 1786). Decoration of this type had been made since the 13th century. It is also known as reverse foil engraving.

3. T. A. Malinina, "The Glass Factory of Prince G. Potemkin-Tavrichesky," in *Imperial Glass Factory, 1777–1917: 225th Foundation Day Anniversary*, exhibition catalog, St. Petersburg: Slaviia, 2004, pp. 25–26. In Russian and English.

4. N. Kachalov, *Steklo*, Moscow: Ied-vo Akademii Nauk SSSR, 1959, p. 251.

5. *Un âge d'or des arts décoratifs, 1814–1848: Galeries Nationales du Grand Palais, Paris, 10 octobre–30 décembre 1991*, exhibition catalog, Paris: Réunion des Musées Nationaux, 1991, passim.

6. Yolande Amic, *L'Opaline française au XIXᵉ siècle*, Paris: Gründ, 1952, p. 146.

7. Fernando Montes de Oca, *L'Age d'or du verre en France, 1800–1830: Verreries de l'Empire et de la restauration*, Paris: the author, 2001, pp. 444 and 457–459.

8. *Ibid.*, p. 266.

9. *Ibid.*, p. 268.

10. Louis-Etienne-François Héricart de Thury, *Rapport du jury d'admission des produits de l'industrie . . .*, Paris: C. Ballard, 1819, p. 237.

11. *Ibid.*, p. 238. "La Reine d'Etrurie" may refer to the wife of Louis de Bourbon, the grand duke of Tuscany.

12. *Nouvelles acquisitions du département des Objets d'art, 1985–1989*, Musée du Louvre, Paris: Réunion des Musées Nationaux, 1990, p. 222.

13. E. Jouy, *Etat actuel de l'industrie française . . .*, Paris: Chez L'Huillier, 1821, p. 75.

14. *Un âge d'or des arts décoratifs* [note 5], pp. 37–38.

15. Héricart de Thury [note 10], p. 238.

16. L. Feduchi, *Colecciones reales de España: El mueble*, [Madrid]: Editorial Patrimonio Nacional, 1965, pp. 372, 458, and 481.

17. *Important French Furniture, Decorations and Clocks*, sale catalog, New York: Sotheby Parke Bernet Inc., November 6, 1982, no. 145.

18. *Un âge d'or des arts décoratifs* [note 5], pp. 133–135.

19. Great Exhibition of the Works of Industry of All Nations (1851), *Official Descriptive and Illustrated Catalogue*, London: Spicer Brothers, 1851, v. 2, p. 701.

20. *Cassell's Illustrated Family Paper Exhibitor . . . of All the Principal Objects in the International Exhibition of 1862*, London: Cassell, Petter, & Galpin, 1862, p. 205. One colored chandelier

dating from the 1790s is pictured in Martin Mortimer, *The English Glass Chandelier*, Woodbridge, Suffolk: Antique Collectors' Club, 2000, pp. 38–39 and 191. It is apparently unique. There are a few other examples with colored drops made before 1851, but they were obviously unusual.

21. London International Exhibition (1862), *The Record of the International Exhibition, 1862*, gen. ed. Robert Mallet, Glasgow: W. MacKenzie, [1862], p. 409.

22. *Rapports du Jury Internationale, Groupe III—Classe 19, Les Cristaux, la verrerie et les vitraux, par MM. Didron et Clemandot*, Paris: Imprimerie Nationale, 1880, p. 30.

1. *Cassell's Illustrated Family Paper Exhibitor . . . of All the Principal Objects in the International Exhibition of 1862*, London: Cassell, Petter, & Galpin, 1862, pp. 203–204.

2. London International Exhibition (1862), *The Record of the International Exhibition, 1862*, gen. ed. Robert Mallet, Glasgow: W. MacKenzie, [1862], p. 203.

3. Önder Küçükerman, *A 500 Years' Heritage in İstanbul: The Turkish Glass Industry and Şişecam*, [Istanbul]: Türkiye Şişeve Cam Fabrikalari A. Ş., [1999], p. 149.

4. *Ibid.*, pp. 139–140.

5. The Sheesh Mahal (literally "Palace of Mirrors") was one of the most lavish rooms in an eastern palace. It was decorated throughout with everything from murals to lovely floral designs on the walls that were reminiscent of Mughal *pietra dura*. As the name suggests, the decoration also included exquisitely designed glass and mirrors.

6. For more information on the Indian palaces, see the books written by the maharajah of Baroda, Martinelli and Michell, Michell and Martinelli, and Raulet and Garde that are listed on page 144.

7. The durbar was a festive reception given by a maharajah for his subjects, at which they pledged their fealty to him.

8. In her account of a trip around the world, the American writer Dorothy Dix noted that the ruler of Udaipur "boasts the bluest blue native blood in India, and is called Maharana, which makes him one peg higher than a Maharajah. He is absolute lord over a vast section of country and millions of people, and has an income of six million dollars a year" (*My Joy-Ride round the World*, London: Mills & Boon Ltd., 1922, p. 216).

9. *Manufacture of Ornamental Glass*, London: n.p., 1823, pp. 5 and 7.

10. John P. Smith, *The Art of Enlightenment: A History of Glass Chandelier Manufacture and Design*, London: Mallett, 1994, pp. 36–37.

11. See the books written by the maharajah of Baroda, Martinelli and Michell, and Raulet and Garde that are listed on page 144.

1. John P. Smith, *Osler's Crystal for Royalty and Rajahs*, London: Mallett, 1991, p. 22, from *The Art-Union*.

2. *Ibid.*

3. *Ibid.*, p. 23.

4. Great Exhibition of the Works of Industry of All Nations (1851), *The Crystal Palace Exhibition, Illustrated Catalogue, London, 1851: An Unabridged Republication of The Art-Journal*, New York: Dover Publications Inc., 1970, p. 255.

5. *The Pottery Gazette*, v. 10, no. 106, April 1, 1886, p. 445, reprinted from the *Birmingham Journal*, May 1851.

6. Smith [note 1], p. 21.

7. At the same time that whale oil was used for lighting devices in the United States, the British employed colza oil. In the 1860s, they switched to kerosene, which they called lamp oil.

8. J. B. (John Burley) Waring, *Masterpieces of Industrial Art & Sculpture at the International Exhibition, 1862*, London: Day & Son, 1863, text for pl. 160.

9. Smith [note 1], p. 75.

10. The salaam is a salutation meaning "peace" that is employed especially in Islamic countries. It is performed by bowing very low and placing the right palm on the forehead.

11. Smith [note 1], p. 76.

12. This communication, as well as the letters cited subsequently in this chapter, are thought to have been written by the manager of the Calcutta store. All of the letters appear to be in the same hand. This correspondence is preserved in the Birmingham City Library.

13. At that time, the currency was pounds, shillings, and pence. The amount noted as "16/12/11" represents 16 pounds, 12 shillings, and 11 pence. Twelve pence was equivalent to one shilling, while 20 shillings equaled one pound.

14. North American and European cities were gradually supplied with municipal gas plants (which produced gas from coal), beginning in the 1820s. By the 1860s, gas illumination in urban areas was widespread. However, because of the cost, this technology was not introduced in India until the 1860s. Judging by this letter, the manager of the Osler shop realized that the use of gas was likely to increase. However, outside the largest cities, only the wealthiest could afford this luxury. Several maharajahs constructed their own gas plants in the 1870s.

15. Smith [note 1], p. 34, from *The Art Journal*.

16. The Society of Arts, *Artisan Reports on the Paris Universal Exhibition of 1878*, London: Sampson Low, Marston, Searle & Rivington, 1879, pp. 126–127.

17. *The Pottery and Glass Trades' Journal*, v. 1, no. 7, July 1878, p. 99.

18. *Ibid.*, v. 1, no. 8, August 1878, p. 116.

19. *Artisan Reports* [note 16].

20. *The Pottery and Glass Trades' Journal*, v. 1, no. 9, September 1878, p. 150.

21. *Crockery and Glass Journal*, v. 7, no. 8, May 2, 1878, p. 8.

22. Robert W. Edis, *Decoration & Furniture of Town Houses*, New York: Scribner and Welford, 1881, pp. 262–263.

23. Paris Exposition Universelle (1878), *The Illustrated Catalogue of the Paris International Exhibition, 1878*, London: Virtue, 1878, p. 142.

24. *Ibid.*, p. 170.

25. Smith [note 1], p. 77, citing the *Indian Daily News* (Calcutta), December 4, 1883.

26. The hookah is a tobacco pipe with a long, flexible tube by which the smoke is drawn through a jar of water and thus cooled.

27. Chutney is a sweet and sour sauce or relish of eastern Indian origin. It is made from fruits, herbs, and other ingredients, with spices and other seasoning.

28. The dated designs are not always in chronological order, so it is impossible to guess at the dates of most of the undated designs.

29. *The Pottery Gazette*, v. 8, no. 80, February 1, 1884, p. 188.

30. *Court Journal*, n.d., clipping in company scrapbook.

CHAPTER 4
Jonas Defries & Sons
PAGES 94–109

1. *The Pottery Gazette*, v. 4, no. 39, September 1, 1880, p. 540.

2. *Cassell's Illustrated Family Paper Exhibitor . . . of All the Principal Objects in the International Exhibition of 1862*, London: Cassell, Petter, & Galpin, 1862, pp. 204–205.

3. London International Exhibition (1862), *The Illustrated Catalogue of the Industrial Department*, London: Printed for Her Majesty's Commissioners, [about 1862], p. 77.

4. *Cassell's* [note 2], pp. 205–206.

5. London International Exhibition (1862), *The Record of the International Exhibition, 1862*, gen. ed. Robert Mallet, Glasgow: W. MacKenzie, [1862], p. 409.

6. This term is discussed on page 20.

7. London International Exhibition (1862), *Reports by the Juries of the International Exhibition, London, 1862*, London: published for the Society of Arts by William Clowes and Son, 1863, p. 367.

8. *Cassell's* [note 2], p. 206.

9. Paris Exposition Universelle (1867), *The Illustrated Catalogue of the Universal Exhibition, Published with the Art Journal*, London and New York: Virtue, [1868], p. 51.

10. *The Era*, October 16, 1864.

11. G. L. M. Strauss and others, *England's Workshops*, London: Groombridge and Sons, 1864, pp. 203–204.

12. *Ibid.*, p. 204.

13. J. Defries & Sons, *New Designs for Glass Chandeliers, Candelabra, Brackets, Pendants, Lanterns, Globes, &c. for 1869 and '70*, [London, 1869], p. [2].

14. *Ibid.*, p. [55].

15. Letter from Osler's Calcutta office (unsigned) to Follett Osler, June 18, 1868.

16. *The Pottery Gazette* [note 1].

1. Jason Ellis, *Glassmakers of Stourbridge and Dudley, 1612–2002: A Biographical History of a Once Great Industry*, Harrogate, England: the author, 2002, pp. 202–207.

2. John Smith, "Glass Furniture in the Nineteenth and Early Twentieth Centuries," *The Journal of The Glass Association*, v. 4, 1992, pp. 21–24.

3. *American Pottery & Glassware Reporter*, v. 9, May 17, 1883. From the J. Stanley Brothers archives in the collection of the Juliette K. and Leonard S. Rakow Research Library, The Corning Museum of Glass.

4. For more information about the *borne*, see Siegfried Giedion, *Mechanization Takes Command: A Contribution to Anonymous History*, New York and London: W. W. Norton & Company, 1948, pp. 371 (illus.) and 374–375.

5. *The Pottery Gazette*, v. 8, no. 84, June 2, 1884, p. 643.

6. *Ibid.*, v. 8, no. 90, December 1, 1884, p. 1366.

1. *The Illustrated London News*, v. 27, no. 769, November 10, 1855, p. 561.

2. Dany Sautot, *Baccarat: Une manufacture française*, Paris: Massin, 2003, p. 97.

3. The howdah was a seat, commonly equipped with a railing and canopy, that was placed on the back of an elephant.

4. Princesse J. L. de Faucigny-Lucinge, "Chez la Bne E. d'Erlanger," *Art et Industrie*, February 1927, pp. 19–23. Of the two tables that are known today, one has a marble top and the other has a glass top. This leads to the conclusion that there may have been a third table, which also featured a glass top. It was customary for glass factories to make copies of specially ordered large pieces that could easily be destroyed. French tables were pressed and then cut, so it would have been easy to press the pieces needed for a third table and have them ready in case they were needed. In 1988, Baccarat re-created two of these tables from the old molds, and both of them had a marble top.

1. *Die Bilanz meines Lebes*, part 2, Palme manuscript no. 1378, Národní Technické Muzeum, Prague.

2. The company was owned by three Palme brothers. Franz and Adolf were the firm's designer and treasurer respectively.

3. This chair, along with other glass furniture, was shown at the Paris International Exhibition of 1937 in a "Boudoir de verre," located in the Czechoslovakian section.

1. John Smith, "Glass Furniture in the Nineteenth and Early Twentieth Centuries," *The Journal of The Glass Association*, v. 4, 1992, p. 21. This source does not supply the date of Lutyens's visit to Udaipur, but he is known to have traveled in 1912 to Delhi, where he designed a building.

2. See chapter 2, note 8.

3. Dorothy Dix, *My Joy-Ride round the World*, London: Mills & Boon Ltd., 1922, p. 218.

Index

Acknowledgments

Many people assisted me in researching this book. John P. Smith, formerly of Mallett & Son (Antiques) Ltd., London, shared his research notes with me. Glennys Wild of the Birmingham Museum and Art Gallery helped me in studying the Osler archives in Birmingham. Michaela Lerch, the curator of the museum at the Cristalleries de Baccarat, checked facts and located pictures. Capt. Amarinder Singh, chief minister of the Punjab, and the royal families of Gwalior, Patiala, and Udaipur allowed us to visit, and to research and photograph their glass. It was a great privilege for me to see their glass and their palaces. Shivdular Dhillon, additional district commissioner, assisted with our visit to Patiala and with research after I returned home. V. S. Indulkar, honorary chief secretary to H. H. Maharajah Scindia and curator of the Jai Vilas Palace in Gwalior, and Gajinder Singh, curator of the crystal gallery at the City Palace, Udaipur, assisted us in photographing the palaces and their collections. Önder Küçükerman shared both his knowledge of the glass in the national palaces of Turkey and his photographs with me. Eva Rydlová in the Czech Republic helped us to secure photographs of the Palme furniture. My heartfelt thanks to all of them.

At The Corning Museum of Glass, Gail Bardhan of the Rakow Research Library hunted endlessly to track down obscure pieces of information, and Jill Thomas-Clark and Mary Chervenak worked diligently to find photographs. Andrew Fortune, a Museum photographer, accompanied me to India and took many of the pictures in the book. Richard Price, the Museum's editor, kept me on track, and Jacolyn Saunders produced a beautiful book design within a limited time frame, for which I am grateful.

This book was originally designed to accompany a special exhibition, "Glass of the Maharajahs," presented at The Corning Museum of Glass during the summer of 2006. I am grateful to the lenders to the exhibition: the Birmingham Museum and Art Gallery, the Cristalleries de Baccarat, Mrs. Gordon Getty, Susan Lynch, the Newport Restoration Foundation, the Patiala Museum, Christopher Vane Percy, Mrs. Prema Dhatri Rao, and the Sklářské Muzeum in Kamenický Šenov. Aseem Sharma of Corning Incorporated aided us in managing the procedures required by the Indian government, John P. Smith helped me locate the objects in private collections, and Poonam Prasad assisted me with all of my contacts in India. I could not have created the exhibition without them.

Picture Credits

The Corning Museum of Glass and the author thank the following for their kind permission to reproduce photographs: Marella Rossi and Barbara Hottinguer of Aveline; Michaela Lerch, curator at Baccarat; Alicia Bradley of the Birmingham Museums and Art Gallery Picture Library; Anne Garde; Amy Stidwell, visual resources manager of Hillwood Museum & Gardens; Prof. Önder Küçükerman, head of the Department of Industrial Design, Mimar Sinan University; Antonio Martinelli; Dr. Jitka Zamrzlová of the Národní Technické Muzeum; Hugh Alexander, deputy manager of the Image Library, The National Archives U.K.; Dr. Cemal Oztaş, president, and Candan Sezgin, assistant director, of The Department of National Palaces; A. Bruce MacLeish, curator, and Michele K. Musto, assistant curator, of the Newport Restoration Foundation; private collection; John P. Smith; and Iraida Bott, deputy director for research, the State Museum "Tsarskoye Selo." We are indebted to Capt. Amarinder Singh, chief minister of the Punjab, and the royal families of Gwalior and Udaipur for most graciously inviting us to visit the palaces and for granting unrestricted permission to photograph the glass furnishings there.

The numbers below refer to pages, except where specified.

Aveline, Paris, France: 17.

Baccarat, Baccarat, France: © Baccarat, 118, 120 (fig. 6-4), 121, 124–126.

Birmingham Museums and Art Gallery, Birmingham, England: 58–61, 68 (fig. 3-19b), 69 (fig. 3-20b), 74–76, 78–83, 84 (fig. 3-35a), 85, 86, 87 (fig. 3-38b), 88–90.

The Corning Museum of Glass, Corning, New York: 12, 73, 77, 91–93, 102–103, 127; photo by Andrew M. Fortune, 36, 38, 39, 45–48, 62, 63, 65 (fig. 3-15), 67, 68 (fig. 3-19a), 72 (fig. 3-24), 84 (fig. 3-35b), 87 (fig. 3-38a), 113–115.

© Anne Garde, Paris, France: 40–41, 44, 65 (fig. 3-16), 66, 69 (fig. 3-20a).

For Further Reading

Allan, Charles and Sharada Dwivedi. *Lives of the Indian Princes.* London: Century Pub. in association with the Taj Hotel Group, 1984.

Baroda, Maharaja of. *The Palaces of India.* New York: The Vendome Press, 1980.

Danny Lane: Breaking Tradition. London: Mallett & Son (Antiques) Ltd., 1999. Catalog of 1999 London exhibition that included 19th-century glass furniture by F. & C. Osler, with text by John P. Smith.

Devi, Gayatri. *A Princess Remembers.* Philadelphia: Lippincott, 1976.

Küçükerman, Önder. *A 500 Years' Heritage in İstanbul: The Turkish Glass Industry and Şişecam.* [Istanbul]: Türkiye Şişeve Cam Fabrikalari A. Ş., [1999].

Martinelli, Antonio and George Michell. *Princely Rajasthan: Rajput Palaces and Mansions.* New York: The Vendome Press, 2004.

Michell, George and Antonio Martinelli. *The Royal Palaces of India.* London: Thames and Hudson, 1994.

Raulet, Sylvie and Anne Garde. *Maharajas' Palaces: European Style in Imperial India.* New York: The Vendome Press, 1996.

Smith, John P. *Osler's Crystal for Royalty and Rajahs.* London: Mallett, 1991.